MOJI BALOGUN ETTI

BEAUTY
from
ASHES

BLUEROSE PUBLISHERS
India | U.K.

Copyright © Moji Balogun-Etti 2024

All rights reserved by author. No part of this publication may be reproduced, stored in a retrieval system or transmitted in any form or by any means, electronic, mechanical, photocopying, recording or otherwise, without the prior permission of the author. Although every precaution has been taken to verify the accuracy of the information contained herein, the publisher assumes no responsibility for any errors or omissions. No liability is assumed for damages that may result from the use of information contained within.

BlueRose Publishers takes no responsibility for any damages, losses, or liabilities that may arise from the use or misuse of the information, products, or services provided in this publication.

For permissions requests or inquiries regarding this publication, please contact:

BLUEROSE PUBLISHERS
www.BlueRoseONE.com
info@bluerosepublishers.com
+91 8882 898 898
+4407342408967

ISBN: 978-93-5989-324-2

Cover design: Shivam
Typesetting: Namrata Saini

First Edition: February 2024

Contents

Part One 1

    Chapter One: Introduction 3

    Chapter Two: The Physics of Vulnerability 13

    Chapter Three: Embracing Disappointment and Failure 28

Part Two 45

    Chapter Four: Owning Your Stories 47

    Chapter Five: From Heartbreak to Healing 59

    Chapter Six: Mental Health and Healing 85

    Chapter Seven: Religion and Resilience 107

Part Three 123

    Chapter Eight: The Journey of Rejection: Navigating Life's Heartaches 125

    Chapter Nine: Writing a Daring New Ending 139

    Chapter Ten: The Beauty that Emerges from within 163

    Daily Affirmation 167

Part One

Chapter One

Introduction

In Beauty from the Ashes, we will embark on a transformative journey, guided by the principles of resilience, vulnerability, and the power of storytelling. Through the lens of personal stories and experiences, we will explore the depths of human emotions and the incredible capacity for growth that resides within us all. This book aims to inspire and empower readers to rise strong, embrace their vulnerabilities, and craft a future filled with beauty and resilience.

In the vast tapestry of human existence, the pursuit of beauty has been an enduring and universal aspiration. From the dawn of time, across cultures and civilizations, the concept of beauty has held a profound place in the human psyche. It's a notion that transcends the superficial, reaching deep into the core of our being, where our innermost desires for transformation and resilience reside. This book, "True Beautiful from the Ashes," invites you to embark on a profound exploration of beauty—one that goes far beyond the mere aesthetics of appearance. It's a journey into the very essence of what it means to be human.

Exploring the Concept of Beauty

"Everything has beauty, but not everyone sees it." - Confucius

What is beauty? It's a question that has perplexed philosophers, artists, and thinkers for centuries. Is beauty merely skin deep, a surface-level quality that can be captured in a fleeting moment, or is it something more profound? As we begin our journey, we must first unravel the intricate threads of this elusive concept.

Beauty is not a fixed or one-size-fits-all attribute; it's a fluid and deeply personal experience. It can manifest in the graceful curve of a smile, the vibrant colours of a sunset, the elegance of a well-composed piece of music, or the resilience of a spirit that refuses to surrender to adversity. True beauty is multifaceted, ever-changing, and, most importantly, it resides within each of us.

Our exploration of beauty will not be confined to the conventional definitions that grace glossy magazines or adorn billboards. Instead, we will delve into the beauty that emerges from the depths of the human soul, forged through the fires of adversity and transformed into something remarkable. We will redefine beauty as an inherent quality of the human spirit—an intrinsic attribute that can shine even in the darkest of times.

What is beauty? To understand the essence of beauty, we must embark on a philosophical and introspective journey that transcends the confines of the superficial and the transient. It is a concept that has been contemplated by thinkers and artists throughout history, and while the answers may vary, the underlying theme remains constant: beauty is a profoundly human experience that touches our souls, stirs our emotions, and shapes our perceptions of the world.

At its core, beauty is a subjective and deeply personal phenomenon. It defies rigid definitions and arbitrary standards, for it exists in the eye of the beholder. What one person finds beautiful, another may not. This subjectivity is what makes beauty such a rich and diverse concept.

Beauty encompasses both the tangible and the intangible. It is found in the elegance of a perfectly symmetrical face, the graceful lines of a work of art, the harmonious melodies of a piece of music, and the serenity of a natural landscape. Yet, it also resides in the kindness of a stranger, the resilience of an individual facing adversity, and the unspoken connections that bind us to one another.

True beauty is not bound by age, gender, race, or any other societal construct. It transcends these boundaries, inviting us to recognize the beauty that exists within every individual. It is a celebration of uniqueness and diversity, a reminder that each of us carries our own story, our own scars, and our own strengths.

As we explore the concept of beauty, we must also acknowledge its impermanence. Beauty is ever-changing, fleeting, and ephemeral. The beauty of youth gives way to the wisdom of age. The vibrant colours of spring transform into the muted tones of winter. The lustre of a momentary triumph fades with the passage of time. Yet, it is within this impermanence that the true essence of beauty is revealed.

Beauty, in its most profound form, emerges from the crucible of life's trials and tribulations. It is not a passive state but an active process—a journey that requires us to confront our vulnerabilities, navigate the depths of our emotions, and find resilience in the face of adversity. It is a journey that transforms us from within, moulding us into individuals who radiate a beauty that transcends the superficial.

In the pages of this book, we will delve deeper into the multifaceted nature of beauty. We will explore how beauty can be a source of inspiration, healing, and transformation. We will witness how individuals have harnessed their inner beauty to overcome the harshest of circumstances, turning their stories of hardship and despair into tales of triumph and resilience.

Our exploration of beauty will take us on a quest to uncover its various dimensions—the beauty of vulnerability, the beauty of resilience, the beauty of compassion, and the beauty of authenticity. Through the stories and experiences shared within these pages, we will come to understand that beauty is not an external quality to be pursued but an internal force waiting to be embraced.

In the chapters that follow, we will journey through the ashes of adversity, guided by the promise of transformation. We will discover that the truest and most enduring beauty is not found in the absence of hardship but in the courage to rise from the ashes and embrace the fullness of our humanity. So, let us embark on this exploration together, as we seek to unveil the profound and ever-evolving concept of beauty that resides within us all.

The Ashes of Adversity

Life, as we know it, is a journey riddled with challenges, trials, and tribulations. Adversity, like a relentless force of nature, can sweep us off our feet, leaving us in the ashes of our own despair. It is in these moments of despair and desolation that we often find ourselves at our most vulnerable. Yet, it is also in these moments that the seeds of transformation are sown.

The ashes of adversity are not a place of finality; they are the fertile ground from which resilience and growth can sprout. Think of a phoenix, rising from its own ashes, reborn in a blaze of glory. Our lives, too, can follow this cyclical pattern of destruction and renewal. It is during the darkest hours, when all hope seems lost, that the human spirit can summon its most extraordinary strength.

In this book, we will explore the profound stories of individuals who have faced insurmountable odds, who have been reduced to ashes by life's trials, and who have emerged from those very ashes, stronger and more beautiful than ever before. Their journeys will serve as beacons of hope, guiding us through the tumultuous terrain of adversity towards the promise of transformation.

Life, with all its complexities and uncertainties, is a relentless journey through terrain both fertile and desolate. At some point, we all find ourselves in the shadow of adversity, facing challenges that seem insurmountable. These moments of despair, where hope appears to be extinguished, are the ashes of our lives. It is here, in the midst of these ashes, that we often discover the truest test of our resilience and our capacity for transformation.

Adversity takes many forms. It can be the loss of a loved one, the collapse of a dream, the sting of rejection, the weight of mental health struggles, or the burden of past mistakes. Adversity does not discriminate; it touches the lives of people from all walks of life, regardless of age, background, or circumstance. It is a universal experience that unites us in our shared humanity.

The ashes of adversity are not a destination but a crucible—a place of reckoning where we confront our deepest fears, vulnerabilities, and limitations. It is in this crucible that we are stripped bare, laid bare before ourselves and the world. In these moments, we often find ourselves at our most vulnerable, but vulnerability is not a weakness; it is the wellspring of our resilience.

Consider the phoenix, a mythical bird that, after being consumed by flames, rises anew from its own ashes. In our own lives, we too can experience a rebirth, a transformation, and a re-emergence from the ashes of adversity. This is the essence of resilience—an innate human quality that allows us to bounce back, to endure, and to thrive in the face of life's harshest trials.

Resilience is not a fixed trait; it is a skill that can be cultivated and honed. It involves the ability to adapt to adversity, to learn from setbacks, and to find strength in vulnerability. It is the capacity to endure suffering without losing hope, to persist in the face of challenges, and to emerge from the ashes stronger and wiser than before.

In this book, we will journey alongside individuals who have faced adversity in its various forms. We will listen to their stories of despair and hopelessness, of being reduced to ashes by life's trials. Yet, we will also witness their remarkable resilience, their unwavering determination to rise from the ashes, and their transformation into individuals of extraordinary strength and beauty.

These stories will serve as guiding lights, illuminating the path from despair to resilience and ultimately to transformation. They will show us that adversity, far from being a final verdict, is merely a chapter in our life's narrative—a chapter that can be rewritten, reimagined, and reshaped.

The ashes of adversity, as dark and suffocating as they may seem, hold within them the embers of resilience and the potential for transformation. They are not the end of our story but the crucible in which we forge the strength to continue. It is through this crucible that we discover the profound truth that beauty is not diminished by adversity; rather, it is often born from it.

The Promise of Transformation

Every trial we face, every hardship endured, and every setback encountered carries with it the promise of transformation. It is the innate human capacity to adapt, evolve, and thrive in the face of adversity that sets us apart as a species. This promise of transformation is not reserved for a select few; it is a birth right that belongs to every individual willing to embrace it.

Transformation is not a linear process; it's a complex interplay of growth, setbacks, and breakthroughs. It's a journey that demands courage, vulnerability, and a willingness to confront our deepest fears and insecurities. It is through this process of transformation that we discover our true selves—the beauty that resides within us, waiting to be unleashed.

As we embark on this transformative journey, we will navigate the uncharted territory of vulnerability, resilience, and the power of owning our stories. We will delve into the depths of disappointment, failure, and heartbreak, unearthing the lessons they hold. We will explore the profound connection between mental health, forgiveness, and the ability to rise from the ashes of our past.

In "Becoming Beautiful from the Ashes," we will venture into the intricate terrain of human existence, where beauty is not a destination but a continuous, ever-unfolding process. It is a journey that beckons us to rise from the ashes of our own experiences, to embrace vulnerability as a source of strength, and to discover the beauty that has been within us all along.

Join us as we embark on this odyssey of self-discovery, resilience, and transformation. Together, we will explore the depths of the human spirit and uncover the extraordinary beauty that emerges from the ashes of adversity.

The concept of transformation is a beacon of hope that has illuminated the darkest corners of human existence throughout history. It is a promise, a potential waiting to be realized, and a testament to the remarkable capacity for change that resides within each one of us. As we delve deeper into the exploration of transformation, we uncover a powerful truth: that our ability to rise from adversity and evolve into our best selves is not only attainable but inherent to our human experience.

Transformation is not a distant ideal or a fleeting moment of change; it is a continuous, lifelong journey. It is the process of shedding old layers, breaking free from limitations, and expanding our horizons. It is the chrysalis from which the butterfly emerges, the phoenix that rises from the ashes, and the dawn after the darkest night. It is the promise that our lives can be rewritten, that our stories can be retold, and that our potential is boundless.

In the pursuit of transformation, we must acknowledge that it is not a linear path, nor is it without its challenges. It often involves a dance with discomfort, a confrontation with our own vulnerabilities, and a willingness to venture into uncharted territories of the self. It is a process that demands courage, resilience, and an unwavering belief in our own capacity for growth.

Transformation is not limited to the physical realm; it extends to our thoughts, emotions, beliefs, and relationships. It invites us to examine our inner landscapes, to question our assumptions, and to challenge the narratives that have held us back. It is a call to evolve not only in how we see ourselves but also in how we interact with the world around us.

One of the most profound aspects of transformation is its intimate connection with vulnerability. It is through vulnerability—the willingness to expose our true selves, warts and all—that we find the fertile ground for growth. Vulnerability is not a sign of weakness but a testament to our authenticity. It is the willingness to say, "This is who I am, imperfections and all," and to embrace the uncertainty that comes with it.

As we journey through the chapters of this book, we will encounter individuals who have harnessed the promise of transformation in their lives. We will witness their struggles, their triumphs, and the profound shifts that have occurred within them. Their stories serve as testament to the inherent human potential for growth, resilience, and beauty.

We will explore the transformative power of vulnerability, the courage it takes to confront our own limitations, and the wisdom that emerges from adversity. We will delve into the depths of disappointment, failure, and heartbreak, recognizing that these experiences, far from being roadblocks, are catalysts for growth.

Additionally, we will explore the intricate relationship between mental health and transformation. We will uncover how individuals have navigated the challenging terrain of depression, anxiety, and other mental health struggles, finding a path towards healing and personal growth.

Also, we will embrace the promise of transformation as an ever-present force in our lives. We will come to understand that beauty is not a fixed destination but a continuous journey—a journey that beckons us to rise from the ashes of our past, to embrace vulnerability as a source of strength, and to recognize that the truest and most enduring beauty is not found in perfection but in the process of becoming. Together, we will embark on this transformative odyssey, unearthing the beauty that resides within us all.

******

Chapter Two

The Physics of Vulnerability

Vulnerability as the Catalyst for Change

Unmasking the Power Within

Vulnerability, often misunderstood and underestimated, is a profound force that holds the key to transformation and personal growth. It is the courageous act of exposing our true selves, embracing our imperfections, and allowing ourselves to be seen, warts and all. In this section, we will delve into the depths of vulnerability and explore how it serves as a potent catalyst for meaningful and lasting change in our lives.

Defining Vulnerability

Before we can fully appreciate the role of vulnerability as a catalyst for change, it's essential to define what vulnerability truly means. Vulnerability is not a sign of weakness, nor is it synonymous with passivity. Instead, it is an act of courage—an intentional choice to show up authentically, even when it feels uncomfortable or risky.

According to Brené Brown, a renowned researcher and author on vulnerability, defines it as "uncertainty, risk, and emotional exposure." It's the willingness to let go of our carefully crafted masks and shields and to allow ourselves to be truly seen by others. Vulnerability is about opening ourselves up to the possibility of rejection, criticism, or disappointment, all while recognizing that it is through this very process that we can experience profound growth and connection.

The Catalyst for Change

Vulnerability is not merely an abstract concept; it is a catalyst for tangible, transformative change in our lives. Here's how vulnerability can act as a powerful force for change:

Embracing Authenticity: When we allow ourselves to be vulnerable, we strip away the façade of perfection and embrace our authentic selves. This authenticity is the foundation upon which personal growth is built. It allows us to acknowledge our flaws, confront our limitations, and recognize our potential for change.

Fostering Connection: Vulnerability is the bridge that connects us to others on a deeper level. When we share our true selves, our fears, and our insecurities, we invite others to do the same. This fosters genuine connections and meaningful relationships, which in turn provide support and encouragement for personal growth.

Learning from Mistakes: Vulnerability enables us to confront our mistakes and failures head-on. Instead of avoiding or denying them, we acknowledge them openly. This willingness to learn from our errors and take responsibility for them is a crucial step in the process of change and self-improvement.

Cultivating Resilience: The act of being vulnerable is in itself an act of resilience. It requires courage and the willingness to face discomfort. Over time, this cultivates emotional resilience, making us better equipped to handle adversity and bounce back from setbacks.

Inspiring Innovation: Vulnerability encourages creative thinking and innovation. It is often through the willingness to take risks and embrace uncertainty that we discover new ideas, solutions, and opportunities for personal and professional growth.

Healing and Emotional Well-being: Vulnerability is an essential component of emotional healing. By acknowledging and expressing our emotions—both the positive and the negative—we create space for healing and personal transformation. It is through vulnerability that we can confront and process past traumas and emotional wounds.

The Paradox of Vulnerability

While vulnerability can be a powerful catalyst for change, it also involves a paradox. It requires us to be open to the possibility of pain and discomfort while simultaneously providing a path to healing and growth. It challenges us to confront our fears and insecurities, even as it offers the potential for liberation from their grip.

Embracing vulnerability is not without its challenges, and it may involve stepping into the unknown, facing rejection, or experiencing discomfort. However, it is precisely in these moments of vulnerability that we often find our greatest opportunities for personal growth and transformation.

In the pages that follow, we will delve deeper into the lived experiences of individuals who have harnessed the power of vulnerability as a catalyst for profound change in their lives. Their stories will illuminate the transformative potential that resides within us all when we have the courage to be vulnerable, authentic, and open to the possibilities of growth, connection, and lasting change.

Vulnerability to Life Experience and Achievement

In the grand narrative of life, vulnerability plays a pivotal role in our pursuit of personal achievement and growth. It is not an abstract concept but a lived experience that has the potential to propel us forward, unlocking doors to personal fulfilment, success, and a deeper understanding of ourselves. Let's explore how vulnerability intertwines with life experiences and how it can be harnessed to achieve our goals and aspirations.

Building Meaningful Relationships

Life is enriched by the depth and quality of our relationships. Vulnerability forms the bedrock of these connections. When we open up to others, sharing our fears, hopes, and dreams, we create a bond built on authenticity. This authentic connection can lead to a support system that is vital for personal achievement. Trusted friends, mentors, or allies can provide guidance, encouragement, and a safety net as we strive to reach our goals.

Overcoming Fear of Failure

Achievement often involves stepping into the unknown, taking risks, and facing the possibility of failure. Vulnerability allows us to confront the fear of failure head-on. When we admit to ourselves and others that we may stumble along the way, we release the paralyzing grip of perfectionism. Embracing vulnerability in our pursuit of achievement means recognizing that setbacks and failures are part of the journey, not the end of it.

Authentic Leadership

In the realm of leadership, authenticity and vulnerability are intertwined. Authentic leaders are relatable, and they acknowledge their vulnerabilities. By doing so, they inspire trust and loyalty among their teams. When leaders are open about their own struggles and challenges, they create a culture where others feel safe to do the same. This fosters innovation, collaboration, and ultimately, achievement within organizations and teams.

Learning and Adaptation

Life is a continuous learning process. Vulnerability allows us to acknowledge what we don't know and to seek growth and improvement. When we admit our limitations and gaps in knowledge, we become open to learning from others, exploring new perspectives, and adapting to changing circumstances. This openness to growth and change is a key ingredient in personal achievement.

Emotional Resilience

Achieving our goals often requires resilience in the face of adversity. Vulnerability is the gateway to emotional resilience. It is through acknowledging and processing our emotions—whether they are feelings of frustration, disappointment, or even fear—that we develop the strength to persevere. Vulnerability enables us to confront challenges with authenticity and grace, ultimately leading to achievement despite the odds.

Self-Discovery and Authentic Goals

Vulnerability invites us to explore our innermost desires, values, and aspirations. It prompts us to question societal expectations and to set goals that align with our true selves. Achieving personal fulfilment and authentic goals—whether in our careers, relationships, or personal endeavors—requires a willingness to be vulnerable in pursuing what truly matters to us.

In essence, vulnerability is not a hindrance to achievement; it is a powerful catalyst that propels us forward. It invites us to embrace our humanity, to connect with others on a deeper level, and to tap into our inner resilience. By weaving vulnerability into the fabric of our life experiences, we can unlock the potential for greater achievement, personal growth, and a richer, more fulfilling journey through life.

John's Journey

Embracing Vulnerability for Personal Transformation

Let's relate the concept of vulnerability as a catalyst for change to a life story.

John's life had been a series of ups and downs, much like anyone else's. He had always been driven by a desire for personal achievement and success, but it seemed like every time he got close to his goals, something would knock him off course. It was in these moments of adversity that John learned the profound power of vulnerability.

The Illusion of Perfection

In his early years, John had believed that achievement meant projecting an image of unyielding strength and competence. He was driven by the fear of failure, and he meticulously crafted a facade of perfection. His friends and colleagues saw a successful, confident individual, but beneath the surface, John was struggling with self-doubt and anxiety.

The Breaking Point

One day, life dealt John a heavy blow. His business, which he had poured his heart and soul into, faced a devastating setback. The financial strain began to take a toll on his mental health, and he felt overwhelmed by the mounting pressure. It was at this breaking point that John realized he could no longer carry the burden alone.

The Turning Point

In a moment of vulnerability, John reached out to his closest friend, Sarah. He admitted his struggles, fears, and doubts. He allowed himself to be seen in his most raw and unfiltered state. To his surprise, Sarah didn't judge him or offer easy solutions. Instead, she listened, empathized, and shared her own vulnerabilities.

Connection and Support

Through this vulnerable conversation with Sarah, John discovered a profound sense of connection and support. He realized that vulnerability was not a sign of weakness but a doorway to authentic relationships. He began to open up to other friends and family members, sharing his challenges and allowing them to do the same. The support he received was transformative.

Resilience and Growth

As John continued to embrace vulnerability, he found himself more resilient in the face of adversity. Instead of seeing setbacks as failures, he viewed them as opportunities for growth. He learned from his mistakes, adapted to changing circumstances, and began to rebuild his business with a newfound sense of authenticity.

Authentic Achievement

Over time, John's definition of achievement shifted. He no longer sought the illusory image of perfection but aimed for goals that resonated with his true self. His journey was marked by authenticity, openness, and a willingness to embrace vulnerability. In this vulnerability, he discovered the strength to not only rebuild his business but to also lead with authenticity, inspiring his team with his resilience and openness.

John's story is a testament to the transformative power of vulnerability in the pursuit of personal achievement. It illustrates how the willingness to be open and authentic can lead to deeper connections, emotional resilience, and the capacity to overcome adversity. In embracing vulnerability, John not only achieved his goals but also found a richer and more fulfilling path through life.

❖ **The Discipline Behind Resilience:**

A Personal Journey of Overcoming Adversity

Let's dive into a life story that highlights the science behind resilience and how it played a pivotal role in one individual's journey of overcoming adversity.

The Unforeseen Challenge

Meet Sarah, a young woman who had always sailed through life with a sense of optimism and ease. She was pursuing her dream career in medicine when she faced an unexpected and life-altering challenge. Sarah was diagnosed with a rare and debilitating chronic illness that threatened to shatter her dreams.

The Emotional Turmoil

In the initial stages of her diagnosis, Sarah felt an overwhelming sense of despair. Her once-promising career prospects seemed dashed, and she was plagued by uncertainty about her future. The emotional turmoil was intense, and Sarah found herself in a deep state of vulnerability.

The Discipline of Resilience

As Sarah navigated the complex emotions brought on by her diagnosis, she began to delve into the discipline behind resilience. She discovered that resilience is not merely a vague concept but a well-researched and understood phenomenon in psychology and neuroscience.

Understanding Resilience Factors

Sarah learned that resilience is not a fixed trait but a dynamic process influenced by various factors:

- ❖ **Positive Relationships:** She understood the importance of social support and leaned on her family and friends for emotional assistance.
- ❖ **Coping Strategies:** Sarah explored different coping strategies, including mindfulness, which helped her manage her stress and anxiety.
- ❖ **Personal Beliefs:** She examined her beliefs and shifted her perspective from **"Why me?"** to "What can I learn from this experience?"

- ❖ **Adaptive Thinking:** Sarah honed her ability to adapt to setbacks, seeing them as opportunities for growth rather than insurmountable obstacles.

Applying Resilience Discipline

Armed with her newfound understanding of resilience, Sarah began to apply these principles to her own life. She sought out support groups for individuals with similar health challenges, forming positive connections with others who shared her experiences. She also worked with a therapist to develop effective coping strategies, such as reframing negative thoughts and setting realistic goals for her recovery.

The Remarkable Transformation

Over time, Sarah's journey unfolded as a testament to the discipline of resilience. She not only managed her chronic illness but also found new purpose in her life. She decided to shift her career focus from clinical practice to medical research, using her experiences to drive her passion for finding solutions to rare diseases.

A Resilient Life

Sarah's life became a living example of the power of resilience. She thrived despite adversity, not in spite of it. She learned that resilience is a dynamic interplay of psychological, social, and cognitive factors that can be cultivated and strengthened through deliberate effort and awareness.

In this life story, we witness the transformative impact of resilience as rooted in scientific understanding. Sarah's journey illustrates how the principles of resilience science can guide individuals through the darkest moments of their lives, helping them not only to overcome adversity but also to emerge from it stronger, more resilient, and with a deeper appreciation for the human capacity for growth and adaptability.

❖ Stories of Triumph Through Vulnerability

The Ascent of a Dreamer

Rachel had always hidden a dream of becoming a renowned chef. With unwavering passion and culinary creativity, she set out to make her mark in the culinary world. She enrolled in cookery school, honed her skills, and worked tirelessly to gain experience in top-tier restaurants.

The Setback That Shook Her World

Despite her dedication and talent, Rachel's dream seemed to be slipping away. She had secured a prestigious position as a sous-chef in a renowned restaurant, only to face a devastating setback. An unexpected accident in the kitchen left her with a severe burn on her dominant hand, rendering her unable to work as a chef.

The Turning Point: A Celebration of Resilience

Rather than allowing the setback to define her, Rachel chose to celebrate her resilience. She understood that her identity was not solely tied to her profession but to her unwavering determination. As she embarked on a journey of physical and emotional healing, Rachel discovered the strength within her that transcended the confines of a kitchen.

A New Cookery Path: A Celebration of Adaptability

While her injured hand healed, Rachel found a new way to express her culinary passion. She started teaching cooking classes and sharing her expertise with others. Through this experience, she not only discovered her talent for teaching but also developed a profound sense of fulfilment in helping others explore their culinary creativity.

A Cookery Success Worth Celebrating

As the years passed, Rachel's story took an unexpected turn. She had not only rebounded from her setback but also found a new culinary path that resonated deeply with her. Rachel became a celebrated culinary instructor, renowned for her ability to inspire others with her resilience and passion.

Celebrating the Lessons from Rachel's Journey

Rachel's journey is a celebration of several profound lessons:

The Resilience Within Us:

Rachel's ability to bounce back was a testament to the resilience that resides within every individual. Her story highlights that setbacks, though painful, can be overcome through determination and a refusal to give up.

The Power of Adaptability:

Rachel's adaptation to a new culinary path showcases the power of adaptability. In celebrating her ability to pivot, we see that sometimes our dreams may evolve in unexpected but equally fulfilling ways.

The Joy of Helping Others

Rachel's newfound passion for teaching celebrates the joy that comes from helping others. Her story reminds us that setbacks can lead to opportunities to make a positive impact on the lives of others.

The Triumph of the Human Spirit

Above all, Rachel's journey is a celebration of the triumph of the human spirit. It emphasizes that success is not limited to a single path and that even in the face of adversity, we can achieve greatness.

In celebrating stories like Rachel's, we honour the resilience, adaptability, and indomitable spirit that define the human experience. Her journey reminds us that failure is not an end but a chance to reinvent ourselves, find new passions, and embrace the transformative power of resilience.

Defying Age Boundaries: Robert's Late-Blooming Triumph

Robert's narrative challenges the notion that age should limit vulnerability and resilience. In his 60s, he decided to pursue a lifelong dream of starting his own business, despite societal expectations that his best years for entrepreneurship had passed. His journey of vulnerability began when he confronted the fear of failure and societal judgments.

This section explores the doubts and uncertainties Robert faced when stepping into the unknown. It delves into the transformation that occurred when he decided to embrace his vulnerability, even at an age when many would hesitate. Robert's story exemplifies the idea that vulnerability is not confined by age and that it can be a driving force for personal growth and resilience, regardless of life stage. Robert's story is a remarkable testament to the notion that age should never be a limiting factor when it comes to vulnerability, growth, and resilience. This section highlight of Robert's late-blooming triumph and the transformative power of embracing vulnerability at any stage in life.

Confronting the Fear of the Unknown

Robert's journey of vulnerability began with a daunting decision – to pursue his lifelong dream of starting his own business. At an age when many would hesitate to take such a risk, Robert confronted the fear of the unknown. This section explores the doubts and uncertainties that clouded his path and examines the inner turmoil he faced when challenging societal expectations.

We delve into Robert's internal dialogue, which oscillated between questioning his abilities and realizing the potential for personal growth. It highlights the courage required to step into uncharted territory, especially at an age when comfort zones often take precedence.

Embracing Vulnerability as a Catalyst for Growth

As Robert pushed past his initial fears and uncertainties, he began to embrace vulnerability as a catalyst for personal and professional growth. This section delves into the transformative process that unfolded as he took risks, made mistakes, and learned from failures.

We explore Robert's experiences of vulnerability in the business world, including moments of self-doubt, financial challenges, and setbacks. Despite these obstacles, Robert's commitment to embracing vulnerability as a means of self-improvement became evident as he navigated the intricacies of entrepreneurship.

Lessons in Resilience and Tenacity

Robert's journey is a testament to resilience and tenacity. This section delves deeper into the challenges he faced along the way, including moments when he considered giving up. It emphasizes the inner strength that emerged as he confronted setbacks and learned to adapt.

We explore how Robert's vulnerability allowed him to seek help and guidance from mentors and peers, demonstrating that vulnerability does not equate to weakness but rather serves as a conduit for growth. His story showcases the unwavering determination that can emerge when one chooses to embrace vulnerability and step beyond age boundaries.

The Fulfilment of Late-Blooming Triumph

Ultimately, Robert's late-blooming triumph became a source of fulfilment that transcended age-related expectations. This section delves into the satisfaction and sense of accomplishment he derived from pursuing his dreams, even in his later years.

We explore Robert's reflections on the transformative power of vulnerability, emphasizing that age should not be a barrier to personal growth and resilience. His story serves as an inspiration to those who may hesitate to embark on new journeys due to societal norms or self-imposed limitations.

The Timelessness of Vulnerability

The conclusion of Robert's narrative reinforces the idea that vulnerability knows no age boundaries. It synthesizes the key takeaways from his late-blooming triumph, emphasizing that embracing vulnerability can lead to personal growth and resilience, regardless of when one chooses to embark on their journey.

Chapter Three

Embracing Disappointment and Failure

Let's delve into the profound lessons that can be learned from disappointment and failure. We explore the transformative power of acknowledging setbacks, share stories of individuals who bounced back after facing adversity, and discuss the importance of cultivating a growth mindset.

❖ The Power of Acknowledging Setbacks:

Disappointment and failure are part and parcel of the human experience. They are not signs of weakness but opportunities for growth and learning. Acknowledging setbacks is the first step towards harnessing their transformative power. When we confront disappointment head-on, we allow ourselves to process the accompanying emotions—frustration, sadness, or even anger. This acknowledgment is not a surrender but an act of resilience.

It is the recognition that setbacks are not final destinations but temporary roadblocks on our journey towards achievement and fulfilment.

A Lesson from Maya's Story

Maya's story exemplifies the transformative power of acknowledging setbacks in the pursuit of personal achievement. By allowing herself to fully experience disappointment and to confront the emotions that came with it, she not only emerged stronger but also achieved her lifelong dream. Her story serves as a testament to the resilience that can be cultivated through the honest acknowledgment of setbacks and the willingness to use them as stepping stones toward greater success.

In our own lives, we can learn from Maya's journey. Acknowledging setbacks is not a sign of weakness but a courageous act that propels us forward. It enables us to process our emotions, learn from our experiences, and ultimately transform setbacks into opportunities for growth and achievement. Maya's story reminds us that setbacks are not the end of our journey; they are, in fact, a vital part of the narrative, shaping us into the resilient individuals we are meant to become.

As Maya's second novel continued to gain popularity, she reflected on the lessons she had learned through the tumultuous journey of acknowledging setbacks.

Resilience is Forged in Adversity

Maya realized that her resilience had been forged in the crucible of adversity. Acknowledging the setback had allowed her to confront her vulnerabilities, process her emotions, and emerge stronger. It was a reminder that setbacks are not roadblocks but opportunities for resilience to shine.

Embracing Vulnerability Leads to Strength

Maya understood that acknowledging her disappointment had required vulnerability. It was through openly expressing her feelings and acknowledging her own human imperfections that she found the strength to bounce back. She had learned that vulnerability is not a weakness but a source of inner power.

Growth is an Ongoing Process

Maya's journey taught her that personal growth is not a one-time event but an ongoing process. Each setback, though painful, had been a catalyst for growth. She realized that the path to achievement was not a straight line but a series of peaks and valleys, with each valley offering an opportunity for self-discovery and improvement.

Success is Defined by Resilience

Maya redefined success in her own terms. It was no longer about external validation or the absence of setbacks; it was about the strength of her resilience. She had learned that true success was not the absence of failure but the ability to rise after each fall, stronger and more determined.

Empathy for Others' Struggles

Maya's journey had also cultivated in her a deep sense of empathy. She understood that everyone faces setbacks in life, and by acknowledging her own, she had developed a greater capacity to empathize with others. Maya became an advocate for sharing stories of resilience and supporting fellow authors who faced rejection and disappointment.

Maya's Legacy

Maya's story continued to inspire countless individuals facing setbacks in various aspects of their lives. She became a symbol of the transformative power of acknowledging setbacks, a beacon of hope for those who needed a reminder that setbacks were not the end but a beginning.

Maya's legacy was not just her literary success but also the resilience she embodied and the lessons she shared with the world. Her story served as a reminder that setbacks were not barriers to achievement but stepping stones to personal growth, strength, and the realization of one's true potential.

Maya's journey, marked by the courageous acknowledgment of her setbacks, illustrated that the power to bounce back and achieve greatness resides within us all. It was a testament to the human spirit's capacity to turn adversity into triumph, and her story continues to inspire others to embrace setbacks as part of their own transformative journeys.

- **Stories of Bouncing Back After Failure**

Throughout history, countless individuals have faced setbacks that could have derailed their dreams, yet they persevered, demonstrating the remarkable capacity of the human spirit to bounce back after failure. These stories serve as beacons of hope and inspiration, showing us that failure is not the end of the road but a stepping stone to success. We'll explore narratives of artists who faced rejection, entrepreneurs who experienced bankruptcy, and athletes who endured defeat, only to rise stronger and more determined than ever. Their stories reveal the resilience that can be cultivated through disappointment and failure.

Stories of Bouncing Back After Failure

Within the tapestry of human existence, stories of individuals bouncing back after failure are woven with threads of resilience, determination, and unwavering belief in the human spirit's capacity to rise. Let's delve into the life story of David, a man whose journey of bouncing back from failure serves as a testament to the extraordinary resilience within us all.

The Ascent

David had always dreamed of becoming an entrepreneur. He envisioned creating a business that would not only bring financial success but also make a positive impact on the world. With boundless enthusiasm, he embarked on his entrepreneurial journey, investing his savings, time, and energy into his start-up venture.

The Setback

However, David's dreams were met with a harsh reality. Despite his relentless efforts, the business faced financial challenges, unexpected setbacks, and fierce competition. After years of hard work, it became evident that the venture was on the brink of failure. David was devastated. He felt like he had let down not only himself but also his family and investors who had believed in him.

The Turning Point

Rather than succumbing to despair, David chose to confront the failure head-on. He acknowledged the pain and disappointment he felt but refused to be defined by them. He sought the counsel of mentors who had experienced their share of business failures. Their stories inspired him to view failure not as an endpoint but as a turning point.

The Resilient Rebound

David decided to pivot. He shifted his focus from his failed venture to a new business idea—one that aligned more closely with his passion and expertise. He poured the lessons learned from his previous failure into this fresh endeavor, determined not to repeat past mistakes.

The Triumph

Years passed, and David's new business flourished. What had initially seemed like a crushing failure had become the stepping stone to his greatest success. He realized that without the lessons learned from his initial setback, he would not have possessed the resilience, adaptability, and wisdom required to achieve his current level of success.

Lessons from David's Journey

David's story reveals several vital lessons about bouncing back after failure:

Resilience in the Face of Adversity

David's ability to bounce back was a testament to his resilience. He demonstrated that setbacks could be temporary and that the strength to overcome them could be cultivated through determination and a refusal to give up.

The Power of Learning

David's failure served as a powerful teacher. He learned invaluable lessons about business, strategy, and adaptability that he would not have encountered without facing adversity. It underscores the idea that failure can be a source of growth and personal development.

The Importance of a Support System

Throughout his journey, David sought guidance and support from mentors and peers. Their stories of overcoming their own failures provided him with encouragement and inspiration. This highlights the importance of seeking support during challenging times.

The Triumph of Persistence

David's ultimate triumph was the result of persistence. He did not let one failure define him or deter him from pursuing his dreams. His story illustrates that success often comes to those who persist in the face of adversity.

In the lives of individuals like David, we see the remarkable potential for growth and transformation that can arise from acknowledging setbacks and bouncing back after failure. Their stories remind us that failure is not a final verdict but a stepping stone on the path to success. It is a testament to the resilience and indomitable spirit of the human experience.

Within the grand tapestry of human existence, there are stories that deserve celebration—narratives of individuals who, after encountering failure, rebounded with extraordinary resilience and determination. Let's embark on a journey to celebrate the life story of Rachel, a woman who defied the odds and transformed her setbacks into stepping stones toward a brighter future.

Celebrating Celebrity Stories of Bouncing Back After Failure

In the realm of celebrity culture, there are tales of stars who have faced adversity, experienced setbacks, and yet managed to rise like phoenixes from the ashes. Let's embark on a journey to celebrate the inspiring story of Sarah, a well-known actress, and how she bounced back after a high-profile failure.

The Ascent to Stardom

Sarah had always harboured a dream of becoming a renowned actress. With undeniable talent and a captivating presence, she pursued her passion with unwavering determination. Her career reached its pinnacle when she landed the lead r

ole in a highly anticipated blockbuster film.

The Setback That Captivated the World

Despite her undeniable talent, Sarah's moment in the spotlight turned into a nightmare. The blockbuster film she had dedicated herself to was critically panned, and her performance was widely criticized. The setback was not just a personal disappointment; it played out on a global stage, with the media and public scrutiny magnified to an unprecedented level.

The Turning Point: A Celebration of Resilience

Rather than succumbing to the weight of public scrutiny, Sarah chose to celebrate her resilience. She acknowledged her disappointment and the vulnerability of the moment. Sarah decided to take a break from the limelight, focusing on self-care, personal growth, and honing her craft.

A New Acting Journey: A Celebration of Reinvention

During her hiatus, Sarah explored diverse acting opportunities, taking on challenging roles in independent films and theatre productions. She chose roles that allowed her to stretch her artistic boundaries and rediscover her love for acting without the glare of the spotlight.

A Triumphant Comeback Worth Celebrating

Years later, Sarah made a triumphant comeback with a critically acclaimed performance in an indie film. Her acting prowess and renewed passion for her craft were celebrated by both critics and audiences. Sarah's journey demonstrated that sometimes, a setback can be the catalyst for a remarkable comeback.

Celebrating the Lessons from Sarah's Journey

Sarah's story is a celebration of several powerful lessons.

The Resilience of the Human Spirit

Sarah's ability to bounce back from a highly publicized failure underscored the incredible resilience that resides within individuals, even in the face of immense pressure and scrutiny.

The Importance of Reinvention:

Her willingness to reinvent herself and explore new creative avenues celebrated the idea that setbacks can lead to opportunities for personal and professional growth.

The Triumph of Artistry

Sarah's triumphant comeback celebrated the enduring power of artistic talent and the capacity for actors to evolve and flourish in their craft over time.

The Inspiration to Others

Sarah's story served as an inspiration to others in the entertainment industry and beyond. It demonstrated that even those in the public eye could experience setbacks and emerge stronger, wiser, and more celebrated than ever.

In celebrating celebrity stories like Sarah's, we are reminded that failure is not a final act but a turning point in the journey of human achievement. Her narrative celebrates resilience, the capacity for reinvention, and the enduring ability of the human spirit to overcome adversity and shine even brighter in the face of setbacks.

❖ Cultivating a Growth Mindset

At the heart of embracing disappointment and failure lies the concept of a growth mindset. Psychologist Carol Dweck coined this term to describe the belief that abilities and intelligence can be developed through dedication and hard work. A growth mindset allows individuals to view challenges as opportunities for growth, rather than as judgments of their innate abilities. Cultivating a growth mindset means reframing setbacks as valuable lessons and viewing effort as a path to mastery. It empowers us to persevere in the face of adversity, to learn from our mistakes, and to continue moving forward on our journey toward our goals.

Now, let us delve deeper into the psychology of disappointment and failure, exploring the emotions they evoke and the resilience they can foster. Through the stories of those who have triumphed over adversity, we'll witness the transformative potential of acknowledging setbacks. We'll also learn practical strategies for cultivating a growth mindset, enabling us to embrace disappointment and failure as integral components of our path to personal and professional achievement.

In our exploration of resilience and achievement, one pivotal element that emerges as a guiding light is the cultivation of a growth mindset. This chapter delves deeper into the transformative power of a growth mindset, drawing upon real-life examples and practical strategies that illuminate the path to resilience and personal accomplishment.

The Essence of a Growth Mindset

At its core, a growth mindset is a belief system that embraces the idea that abilities and intelligence can be developed through dedication, effort, and learning. It contrasts with a fixed mindset, which assumes that abilities are innate and unchangeable. When we cultivate a growth mindset, we open the door to a world of possibilities and personal growth.

Learning from Failure and Setbacks

One of the fundamental principles of a growth mindset is the recognition that failure and setbacks are not indicators of inadequacy but opportunities for learning and growth. Those who possess a growth mindset view challenges and mistakes as stepping stones on the path to mastery. They understand that it's not about avoiding failure but about learning from it.

Carol Dweck's Research

Psychologist Carol Dweck's pioneering research on mindset reveals the profound impact of these beliefs on our lives. Her studies demonstrate that individuals with a growth mindset are more likely to persevere in the face of challenges, take risks, and ultimately achieve higher levels of success.

Real-Life Stories of Growth Mindset in Action

Throughout history, numerous individuals have exemplified the power of a growth mindset in their remarkable journeys. For instance, Thomas Edison, the inventor of the light bulb, famously remarked, "I have not failed. I've just found 10,000 ways that won't work." His relentless pursuit of innovation and his willingness to learn from each "failure" illustrate the essence of a growth mindset.

Similarly, the story of J.K. Rowling, author of the Harry Potter series, reflects the transformative potential of a growth mindset. She faced numerous rejections from publishers but did not give up. Instead, she continued to refine her craft, believing in her ability to grow as a writer. Her eventual success serves as a testament to the resilience that can emerge from embracing a growth mindset.

Practical Strategies for Cultivating a Growth Mindset

Cultivating a growth mindset is not just about adopting a new belief; it requires deliberate practice and the development of certain habits. Here are some practical strategies for fostering a growth mindset:

- ❖ **Embrace Challenges: Seek out challenges that stretch your abilities and provide opportunities for growth.**
- ❖ **View Effort as a Path to Mastery: Emphasize the value of effort and hard work in achieving your goals.**

- ❖ **Learn from Setbacks:** When faced with failure or setbacks, analyze what went wrong and extract lessons for improvement.
- ❖ **Cultivate Curiosity:** Foster a natural curiosity about the world, always seeking to learn and explore new ideas.
- ❖ **Embrace the "Not Yet" Mentality:** Instead of saying "I can't," say "I can't do it yet." This subtle shift in language acknowledges the potential for growth.

In the journey of resilience and personal achievement, cultivating a growth mindset stands as a foundational pillar. It is a belief system that not only empowers us to embrace setbacks as opportunities for growth but also equips us with the determination to pursue our goals with unwavering dedication. Through the stories of individuals who have harnessed the power of a growth mindset, we witness the profound impact it can have on our ability to bounce back from adversity and thrive in the face of challenges.

There are tools you can use for potential mindset growth.

Positive Mindset

- See failure as an opportunity
- Differentiate one problem from others
- Generalizing the causes of bad things
- See the gain
- Make the most of all situations

Negative Mindset

- See failure as loss
- Overgeneralizing problem
- Self-blaming for bad things
- See the pain
- Let situations do their things

GROWTH MINDSET

- ✓ I can learn anything new
- ✓ My effort is the main factor that determines my abilities
- ✓ With each failure, I will learn and get even better
- ✓ I think that feedback is constructive and helpful
- ✓ I really like to try new things

LIMITED MINDSET

- ✗ I'm either good or I'm not
- ✗ My abilities are predetermined by my genes
- ✗ Failure shows me what I'm not good at
- ✗ Feedback is always criticism
- ✗ I don't like to get out of my comfort zone

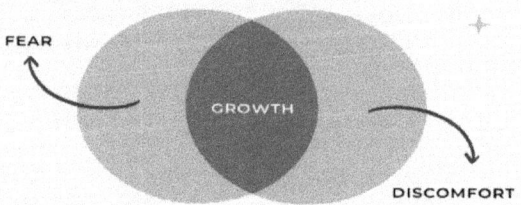

the *magic* HAPPENS OUTSIDE YOUR COMFORT ZONE

Mindset Shifts

This is hard, I can't do it.	→	This is challenging, but growth only comes with challenge.
I've got a long way to go to be the person I want to be.	→	I've come so far and grown so much from who I was.
I'll never reach my goals, my dreams are out of reach.	→	Anything is possible and I can do amazing things, just take it one day at a time.

HOW TO ACHIEVE A MINDFUL MINDSET

Externally

Internally

- Create a mindful environment
- Spend time in nature
- Listen to relaxing Music
- Connect with others
- Journal your thoughts

- Be more confident
- Show kindness
- Love yourself
- Have a plan

- Connect with your values
- Practice gratitude
- Acknowledge your thoughts
- Connect with your Body
- Practice deep breathing

A positive mind finds opportunity in everything

Part Two

Chapter Four

Owning Your Stories

Transforming Vulnerability into Strength

In the journey of personal transformation and resilience, owning our stories emerges as a pivotal chapter. It's a testament to the courage required to confront our truths, overcome the weight of shame and guilt, and ultimately, turn our stories, even the most painful ones, into sources of strength. Vulnerability often comes hand-in-hand with owning our stories. It's the act of opening ourselves up to the possibility of judgment, rejection, or misunderstanding. When we confront our truths, we are exposed in our rawest form. But it's through this vulnerability that we connect with others on a deeper level, forging bonds built on authenticity and shared experiences.

❖ The Courage to Confront Our Truths

Owning our stories begins with the profound act of courage—the willingness to confront our truths, even when they are uncomfortable or painful. It means acknowledging the aspects of our lives that we may have kept hidden, the mistakes we've made, and the vulnerabilities we've tried to shield from the world. This courage is not a denial of our imperfections but an embrace of our humanity. The essence of resilience and personal growth often hinges on our ability to muster the courage required to confront our truths. It's an aspect of the human experience that goes beyond mere acknowledgment; it's about unearthing the depths of authenticity and facing the most profound aspects of our lives head-on.

The Weight of Hidden Truths

Many of us carry within ourselves truths that we've kept hidden, even from our own conscious awareness. These truths may be the memories of past traumas, the pain of unfulfilled dreams, or the guilt associated with our own mistakes. They often lie in the shadows, shaping our behaviors, thoughts, and emotions from the hidden corners of our minds.

The Initial Discomfort

Confronting our truths can be an uncomfortable, even harrowing process. It means stepping out of the comfort zones we've constructed around our identities and facing the aspects of ourselves we'd rather avoid. It might entail admitting to ourselves that we are not infallible, that we've been hurt, or that we've hurt others. The discomfort arises from the fear of judgment, both self-imposed and from others.

The Catalyst for Transformation

Yet, it is precisely in this discomfort that the seed of transformation is planted. Confronting our truths is an act of radical honesty with ourselves. It is a declaration that we are willing to stand in the light of our own existence, acknowledging the beauty and the blemishes, the victories and the defeats. It is an acknowledgment that we are not defined solely by our past but are continuously evolving beings capable of growth and change.

The Empowerment of Authenticity

Confronting our truths empowers us to live authentically. When we carry the weight of hidden truths, we often wear masks to hide our vulnerabilities or to conform to societal expectations. Authenticity, on the other hand, allows us to be true to ourselves, expressing our values, beliefs, and emotions without fear or preteens. It is a source of deep self-respect and personal power.

Self-Awareness

The journey begins with self-awareness. We must first recognize that there are truths within us that need to be confronted. This recognition often arises when we feel the weight of our past or the nagging discomfort of unexpressed emotions.

Acceptance

Acceptance is the bridge that leads us to confront our truths. It involves acknowledging that these truths are a part of who we are and that denying or suppressing them only perpetuates our pain. Acceptance is not about condoning our past actions or experiences but about acknowledging their existence.

Courageous Exploration

The next step is the courageous exploration of our truths. This may involve seeking professional help, engaging in introspective practices like journaling, or engaging in honest conversations with trusted individuals. It requires the willingness to face discomfort head-on.

Self-Compassion

Self-compassion plays a crucial role in this process. It involves treating ourselves with the same kindness and understanding that we would offer to a friend facing a similar situation. Self-compassion reminds us that we are human, imperfect, and deserving of love and forgiveness.

Integration

As we confront our truths, we begin to integrate them into our sense of self. This integration involves recognizing that our truths, even the painful ones, are a part of our life's narrative. They have shaped us but do not define us entirely.

Healing and Transformation

Confronting our truths can be a catalyst for healing and transformation. It allows us to release pent-up emotions, gain perspective on our experiences, and ultimately find meaning and growth in the process. Healing often involves forgiveness, both of ourselves and others.

Case Study:

Viktor Frankl's Search for Meaning:

Viktor Frankl, a Holocaust survivor and psychiatrist, provides a powerful case study in confronting truths. Through the horrors of the concentration camps, Frankl confronted the harsh realities of human suffering and the fragility of life. His experiences led him to develop a profound understanding of the human capacity to find meaning in the face of extreme adversity.

Frankl's courage to confront the truth of his experiences allowed him to transform his suffering into a powerful testament to resilience and the human spirit. His book, "Man's Search for Meaning," has since inspired countless individuals to find purpose and meaning in their own lives, even in the most challenging circumstances.

Finally, through the stories of those who have summoned the courage to confront their truths, we gain inspiration and insight into the profound impact of this journey. It is a testament to the resilience and strength that can be harnessed when we choose to confront our truths and transform vulnerability into a source of personal growth and empowerment

❖ Overcoming Shame and Guilt

Shame and guilt can be formidable barriers on the path to owning our stories. They have the power to paralyze us, making it difficult to confront our truths. However, as researcher Brené Brown emphasizes in her work, shame cannot survive in the presence of empathy and compassion. Overcoming shame and guilt involves self-compassion and the realization that making mistakes or facing adversity is part of the human experience. When we free ourselves from the grip of shame and guilt, we can truly own our stories.

The Weight of Shame and Guilt

Shame and guilt are two distinct yet interconnected emotions that can hold us captive. Shame revolves around a belief that we are fundamentally flawed or unworthy, while guilt is tied to remorse for specific actions or behaviors. Both emotions carry a heavy burden that can erode our self-esteem, inhibit our growth, and even lead to mental health issues if left unaddressed.

The Paralyzing Effect

Shame and guilt have a paralyzing effect, often immobilizing individuals from taking positive actions or confronting their truths. They foster self-doubt, self-criticism, and a perpetual feeling of inadequacy. This emotional baggage can hinder our ability to bounce back from setbacks and embrace resilience.

The Path to Healing

Overcoming shame and guilt is a multifaceted process that involves self-compassion, self-forgiveness, and a deep exploration of the roots of these emotions. It requires a willingness to confront the past, make amends when necessary, and let go of the emotional burdens that have been carried for too long.

The Role of Self-Compassion

Self-compassion is a powerful antidote to shame and guilt. It involves treating oneself with the same kindness and understanding that we would offer to a friend facing similar circumstances. Self-compassion reminds us that we are human, capable of making mistakes, and deserving of love and forgiveness.

Acknowledging and Making Amends

For guilt specifically, acknowledging the actions or behaviors that caused harm and taking steps to make amends can be a crucial part of the healing process. It requires a commitment to learning from past mistakes and a genuine effort to avoid repeating them.

The Courage to Forgive Oneself

Forgiving oneself is often the most challenging step in overcoming shame and guilt. It requires acknowledging the pain we've caused ourselves or others, accepting responsibility for our actions, and letting go of the emotional burdens associated with past mistakes. It is an act of self-compassion that opens the door to healing and growth.

Real-Life Stories of Overcoming Shame and Guilt

This section will not be justified if I failed to mention that the stories of individuals who have triumphed over shame and guilt serve as powerful examples of the transformative potential of this journey.

For instance, the story of Nelson Mandela, who forgave his oppressors and worked toward reconciliation, showcases the liberating power of forgiveness in the face of guilt.

Similarly, the personal journey of Maya Angelou, who overcame a traumatic childhood and found healing through her writing, demonstrates the capacity to rise above shame and transform one's narrative into one of resilience and strength.

Practical Strategies for Overcoming Shame and Guilt:

- ❖ **Self-Compassion:** Practice self-compassion by speaking to yourself with kindness and understanding.

- ❖ **Mindfulness:** Cultivate mindfulness to become more aware of the emotions associated with shame and guilt and to avoid becoming entangled in self-criticism.

- ❖ **Seeking Support:** Seek support from friends, family, or a therapist who can provide empathy and guidance on the journey to healing.

- ❖ **Amends and Restitution:** When appropriate, make amends for past actions and behaviours to address guilt and seek closure.

- ❖ **Therapeutic Intervention:** Consider professional therapy or counselling to explore the roots of shame and guilt and develop strategies for overcoming them.

- ❖ **Breaking the Cycle:** Shame and guilt can become ingrained emotional patterns. Recognizing when you're entering this cycle and consciously choosing a different response is a crucial part of healing. It involves interrupting the automatic negative self-talk and replacing it with self-compassion and positive affirmations.

- ❖ **The Role of Gratitude:** Practicing gratitude can be a powerful tool in overcoming shame and guilt. It shifts your focus from what went wrong to what you have learned and gained from your experiences. Gratitude can help you see the silver linings in even the darkest moments.

- ❖ **The Ongoing Journey:** It's important to acknowledge that overcoming shame and guilt is an ongoing journey. There may be moments when these emotions resurface, but with each recurrence, you become better equipped to handle them with self-compassion and resilience.

The section of overcoming shame and guilt is a testament to the transformative power of self-compassion, forgiveness, and the courage to confront our past. It is a journey that leads us from the depths of emotional burden to the liberation of self-acceptance and resilience. Through the stories of those who have transcended shame and guilt, we find inspiration and guidance on the path to healing, growth, and self-fulfilment.

❖ Turning Our Stories into Strength

Turning our stories into strengths involves the transformative alchemy of storytelling. It's the process of not just acknowledging our past but actively reframing it to find meaning, purpose, and growth. When we tell our stories, we reclaim the narrative, becoming the authors of our own lives. This process can be incredibly empowering, as we move from being passive victims of circumstances to active agents of change.

Real-Life Examples of Owning Our Stories

Countless individuals have demonstrated the power of owning their stories, turning vulnerability into strength. Take the example of Malala Yousafzai, the Pakistani education activist. After surviving a near-fatal attack by the Taliban, she not only confronted the truth of her experience but also used her story to advocate for girls' education worldwide. By owning her story, she transformed her vulnerability into a powerful force for change.

Similarly, the journey of Nelson Mandela from prisoner to president showcases the resilience that arises from owning one's story. He confronted the painful truths of apartheid and emerged as a symbol of reconciliation and forgiveness, showing how even the darkest chapters of our lives can be rewritten with strength and resilience.

Oprah Winfrey, from a challenging childhood marked by poverty and abuse, Oprah turned her story into a source of strength and inspiration. Her resilience, determination, and ability to connect with others through her own experiences propelled her to become a media mogul and advocate for personal growth.

Another inspiring real life story - Nick Vujicic. Without arms and legs, Nick Vujicic transformed his story of physical adversity into a platform for motivational speaking and advocacy. His story has inspired countless individuals to embrace life's challenges with unwavering determination

And of course Stephen Hawking, despite facing a debilitating illness, Stephen Hawking's ground breaking work in theoretical physics continued to inspire the world. His determination to pursue his passion despite immense physical limitations exemplifies the strength that can emerge from personal challenges.

Practical Steps for Owning Our Stories:

❖ **Self-Reflection and Self-Awareness**

The journey begins with self-reflection and self-awareness. It requires us to delve deep into our life experiences, examining how they have shaped us, and identifying the strengths that have emerged from adversity.

❖ **Journaling**

Begin by writing down your thoughts and feelings about your experiences. Journaling can be a safe space to confront your truths.

❖ **Seek Support**

Reach out to friends, family, or a therapist who can provide empathy and understanding as you navigate your story.

❖ Practice Self-Compassion

Be kind to yourself. Understand that making mistakes or facing hardships is part of the human experience, not a reflection of your worth.

❖ Share Your Story

When you're ready, share your story with others, whether through writing, speaking, or art. The act of sharing can be a powerful catalyst for transformation.

❖ Finding Meaning and Purpose

One of the most powerful ways to turn our stories into strengths is by finding meaning and purpose within them. This involves reframing our narratives to see the lessons, growth opportunities, and silver linings that may have emerged from our hardships. It's about understanding that our experiences, no matter how challenging, have contributed to our personal development.

❖ Inspiring Others

Our stories have the power to inspire and uplift others who may be facing similar challenges. When we share our narratives authentically and vulnerably, we create a sense of connection with those who resonate with our experiences. This connection can provide hope, encouragement, and a sense of belonging to others who may be struggling.

❖ Embracing Resilience as a By-product

Resilience is often born from adversity. When we confront and overcome challenges, we develop a resilience muscle that allows us to bounce back from future setbacks with greater ease. Our stories of triumph over adversity become a testament to our resilience and serve as a source of strength when facing new obstacles.

❖ The Role of Self-Identity

Turning our stories into strengths is closely tied to our self-identity. It involves shifting from seeing ourselves as victims of our circumstances to becoming the authors of our own narratives. It's recognizing that our past does not define us but shapes us into who we are becoming.

❖ Reframing and Reshaping Narratives:

Central to this process is the reframing and reshaping of our narratives. Instead of viewing ourselves as victims of circumstance, we become the authors of our own stories. We reinterpret our past, emphasizing the resilience, courage, and growth that emerged from challenges.

❖ Identifying Core Strengths

Our stories often reveal our core strengths and qualities, such as resilience, determination, empathy, and adaptability. Recognizing and embracing these strengths allows us to harness them in our ongoing journey.

In conclusion, turning our stories into strengths is a transformative journey of self-discovery, growth, and resilience. It's about finding meaning, purpose, and inspiration in our experiences, no matter how challenging they may be. When we embrace our narratives as sources of strength, we tap into the alchemy of personal transformation, transmuting life's adversities into the gold of resilience and inner fortitude.

Chapter Five

From Heartbreak to Healing

The Journey of Emotional Recovery

In the human experience, heartbreak is an inevitable companion on our journey. It encompasses grief, loss, and the complex emotions tied to forgiveness and unforgiveness. This chapter will explore the profound journey of emotional recovery, delving into the depths of the human heart as it seeks healing and reconciliation.

❖ **Dealing with Grief and Loss**

Grief is a universal human emotion that accompanies loss. Whether we lose a loved one, a cherished dream, a relationship, or even a part of ourselves, grief becomes the language of the heart in times of sorrow. The journey from heartbreak to healing begins with acknowledging and crossing the ground of grief.

The Multifaceted Nature of Grief

Grief is not a singular emotion but a multifaceted and evolving experience. It can encompass a wide range of emotions, including sadness, anger, guilt, confusion, and even relief. These emotions may come in waves, intensifying at unexpected moments, or gradually subsiding over time.

The Universality of Loss

Loss is an integral part of life. We experience loss not only in death but also in the form of broken relationships, lost opportunities, shattered dreams, and even the passage of time. Recognizing the universality of loss can help normalize the grieving process.

The Role of Time

Time is a critical factor in dealing with grief. Grief does not have a fixed timeline; it varies from person to person and can last weeks, months, or even years. With time, the intensity of grief often lessens, but it may never fully disappear. The goal is not to "get over" grief but to learn to live with it.

Stages of Grief

The stages of grief, as popularized by Elisabeth Kübler-Ross, include:

- ❖ **Denial:** Initially, it can be difficult to accept the reality of the loss. Denial may serve as a protective mechanism, helping individuals gradually come to terms with their new reality.
- ❖ **Anger:** Anger often follows denial as the realization of the loss sets in. People may feel angry at themselves, others, or even the universe for the unfairness of the situation.

- ❖ **Bargaining:** In this stage, individuals may engage in "what if" or "if only" scenarios, trying to negotiate with the past or with a higher power to reverse the loss.
- ❖ **Depression:** This stage is marked by profound sadness and despair. It's a natural response to the pain of loss.
- ❖ **Acceptance:** Acceptance is not about being "okay" with the loss but rather about coming to terms with the reality of it. It's a step toward finding a way to move forward.

It's important to note that these stages are not linear, and individuals may experience them in varying sequences or revisit them multiple times throughout the grieving process.

Coping Mechanisms

People employ various coping mechanisms to deal with grief and loss. Some may seek solace in solitude and introspection, while others find comfort in the company of friends and family. Engaging in creative outlets, such as art, music, or writing, can be therapeutic ways to process emotions.

Support Systems

Support from friends, family, or support groups can be invaluable during the grieving process. Talking about one's feelings, sharing memories, and receiving empathy and understanding from others can provide solace and comfort.

Professional Help

In cases of complicated or prolonged grief, seeking professional help from therapists or grief counsellors may be necessary. These professionals can provide guidance in navigating the complexities of grief and offer tools to cope with its emotional toll.

In conclusion, dealing with grief and loss is a deeply personal journey that unfolds at its own pace. It is a testament to the depth of human emotion and the capacity of the heart to both suffer and heal. While the landscape of grief may be challenging and at times overwhelming, it is also marked by resilience, strength, and the enduring bonds of love and memory. Through the process of dealing with grief.

❖ Forgiveness and Unforgiveness

The landscape of heartbreak is also marked by the complexities of forgiveness and unforgiveness. These emotions hold immense power in shaping our emotional recovery. The intricate interplay between forgiveness and unforgiveness is a pivotal aspect of the human experience, especially in the context of healing and resilience. This section will go deeper into the complexities of these emotions, exploring their profound impact on individuals and their journeys from adversity to flourishing.

The Act of Forgiveness

Forgiveness is often described as a gift one gives to oneself rather than to the wrongdoer. It is an act of releasing resentment, anger, or the desire for revenge. Forgiving does not mean condoning or forgetting the wrongdoing; rather, it involves a conscious decision to let go of the emotional burden associated with it. The act of forgiveness is a transformative process, and it includes the following elements:

- ❖ **Acknowledgment:** Forgiveness begins with acknowledging the pain and hurt caused by the wrongdoing. It requires facing the reality of the situation and the emotions it has stirred.

- ❖ **Empathy:** Empathy plays a crucial role in forgiveness. It involves trying to understand the perspective of the wrongdoer and recognizing that they, too, may have their own pain and struggles.
- ❖ **Compassion:** Compassion towards oneself and the wrongdoer is essential. It entails treating both parties with kindness and understanding, recognizing that holding onto anger and resentment harms one's own well-being.
- ❖ **Release:** Forgiveness is the act of releasing the emotional hold that the wrongdoing has on one's heart and mind. It is freeing oneself from the chains of unforgiveness.

The Weight of Unforgiveness

Unforgiveness, conversely, can be a heavy burden to bear. When individuals choose to hold onto anger, resentment, and a desire for revenge, they often discover that these negative emotions begin to consume them. The weight of unforgiveness can manifest in various ways:

- ❖ **Physical Health:** Holding onto anger and resentment has been linked to physical health problems such as increased stress, high blood pressure, and even heart disease.
- ❖ **Emotional Health:** Unforgiveness can lead to persistent feelings of bitterness, anger, and sadness. It can hinder the process of emotional healing and hinder one's ability to find peace.
- ❖ **Interpersonal Relationships:** The effects of unforgiveness can spill over into personal relationships, causing tension and distance between individuals.
- ❖ **Spiritual and Psychological Well-being:** Unforgiveness can erode one's sense of inner peace

and spiritual well-being. It often keeps individuals locked in a cycle of negativity and pain.

The Complexity of Forgiveness

Forgiveness is not always easy or straightforward. In cases of profound harm or trauma, forgiveness may require significant time and inner work. It is a deeply personal journey, and there is no one-size-fits-all approach to forgiveness. Some individuals may find forgiveness through religious or spiritual beliefs, while others may seek guidance from therapists or counsellors.

The Liberation of Forgiveness

Forgiveness, when achieved, is a profound act of liberation. It signifies a conscious decision to break free from the shackles of unforgiveness and reclaim one's emotional well-being. It is a step toward personal growth, healing, and resilience. Forgiveness, when it occurs, is like to the stars in the night sky—bright points of light that guide the way. It is a testament to the resilience of the human spirit, demonstrating the capacity to transcend pain and anger. Forgiveness is not always granted, nor is it obligatory, but when it does happen, it can be a beacon of hope and reconciliation.

Real-Life Stories of Forgiveness and Unforgiveness

Real-life stories provide poignant examples of the power of forgiveness and the weight of unforgiveness.

Forgiveness: Mary's Journey of Healing

Mary had always been known for her unwavering kindness and compassion. However, her world was shattered when she discovered that her best friend, Sarah, had betrayed her in the most heart-wrenching way possible. The sense of betrayal cut deep, leaving Mary consumed by anger, hurt, and an overwhelming desire for revenge.

In the days following the revelation, Mary's emotions swung like a pendulum. The initial shock gave way to intense anger and bitterness. She couldn't sleep, couldn't concentrate at work, and felt like her life was spiralling out of control. It was during one sleepless night, as tears streamed down her face, that Mary made a decision that would change her life forever.

Mary chose to forgive Sarah.1

This decision didn't come easily. It required immense courage and self-reflection. Mary realized that harboring anger and seeking revenge was only hurting herself. Forgiveness became her path to healing and emotional freedom. She chose to let go of the pain and betrayal, not for Sarah's sake, but for her own.

Over time, Mary's heart began to mend. She rekindled old friendships and found solace in her support network. Her decision to forgive allowed her to regain control of her life and find the strength to move forward. It wasn't an overnight process, but with each passing day, Mary felt lighter and more at peace.

Today, Mary is a beacon of forgiveness and healing. She shares her story with others, inspiring them to choose forgiveness as a path to emotional freedom and personal growth.

Unforgiveness: David's Unyielding Grudge

David had always been known for his stubbornness. He was a proud and principled man who never backed down from a fight. But when a dispute with his brother, Michael, escalated into a bitter feud that spanned years, David's stubbornness took on a darker form – unforgiveness.

The rift between David and Michael originated from a disagreement over the family inheritance. What began as a simple misunderstanding soon devolved into a full-blown family feud. They exchanged harsh words, accused each other of betrayal, and severed all ties.

Years passed, and the feud remained unhealed. David's anger and resentment toward his brother consumed him. He couldn't bear the thought of forgiving Michael, believing it would mean conceding defeat. The bitterness festered within him, affecting his relationships with other family members and friends.

David's unyielding grudge isolated him from those who cared about him most. His anger had become a heavy burden that he carried with him every day. He knew that he had the power to end the feud, but his pride wouldn't allow it. Unforgiveness had become a prison from which he couldn't escape.

The story of David serves as a stark reminder of the corrosive nature of unforgiveness. It's a cautionary tale that illustrates how holding onto grudges can lead to personal isolation and emotional turmoil.

Forgiveness: Sarah's Act of Self-Liberation

Sarah had always been a strong and independent woman. When her long-term relationship came to an abrupt and painful end, she was left with a shattered heart and a profound sense of betrayal. The breakup left her emotionally wounded, and she was consumed by anger and resentment toward her former partner.

In the days and weeks that followed, Sarah found herself replaying the painful events of the relationship in her mind. The anger burned within her, and thoughts of revenge crossed her mind more than once. However, as time passed, Sarah began to realize that holding onto her anger was only causing her more pain.

She came to a transformative realization – forgiveness wasn't about absolving her former partner of wrongdoing;

it was about liberating herself from the emotional burden she carried. Sarah chose to forgive, not for her former partner's sake, but for her own healing and growth.

The journey of forgiveness was not easy. It required introspection and self-compassion. Sarah learned to extend forgiveness as an act of self-liberation. As she forgave, she felt the weight of anger and resentment lift from her shoulders. She found solace in the idea that forgiveness was her path to emotional healing and personal growth.

Today, Sarah stands as a testament to the transformative power of forgiveness. She has rebuilt her life with a newfound sense of strength and resilience. Her story serves as an inspiration to others, reminding them that forgiveness can be an empowering choice, leading to emotional freedom and personal healing.

Unforgiveness: Mark's Relentless Pursuit of Vengeance

Mark had always been a driven and competitive individual. When a professional rivalry escalated into a personal vendetta, it consumed his thoughts and actions for years. His relentless pursuit of vengeance was driven by a desire to prove his superiority and seek retribution against a former colleague, Alex.

The feud between Mark and Alex originated in the competitive world of business. What began as a healthy rivalry soon turned toxic. They engaged in a series of actions aimed at undermining each other's careers and reputations. The pursuit of vengeance became Mark's singular focus, and he spared no effort to exact revenge on Alex.

Years passed, and the feud showed no signs of abating. Mark's obsession with vengeance had taken a toll on his mental health and personal relationships. His friends and family watched helplessly as he became consumed by his desire for retribution. The pursuit of vengeance had become a relentless, all-consuming force in his life.

Mark's story serves as a cautionary tale, illustrating the destructive cycle that unforgiveness can create when it leads to an unrelenting thirst for vengeance. It is a stark reminder of the self-destructive nature of harbouring grudges and the profound toll it can take on an individual's emotional and mental well-being.

Forgiveness: Elena's Healing Through Compassion

Elena's life took a tragic turn when a senseless act of violence shattered her family. A member of her family was a victim of violence, and the pain and trauma reverberated through their lives. In the aftermath of the incident, Elena faced an unimaginable decision – whether to forgive the perpetrator.

The initial shock and anger that consumed Elena were overwhelming. The desire for revenge burned within her, and she longed to see justice served. However, as she navigated the depths of her grief and anger, Elena came to a transformative realization. She realized that forgiveness was her path to healing, not just for herself but for her entire family.

Elena's decision to forgive was not an easy one. It was a process that required immense courage and compassion. She chose to break the cycle of violence that had scarred her family for generations. Through forgiveness, she sought to promote healing, not just for herself but for her family as well.

Over time, Elena's forgiveness became a source of strength and healing for her family. It allowed them to find a measure of closure and begin the process of rebuilding their lives. Elena's story serves as a testament to the remarkable potential of forgiveness, even in the face of profound tragedy.

Unforgiveness: Richard's Prison of Resentment

Richard had always been a private and reserved individual. He was known for holding grudges and rarely letting go of past grievances. One particular incident, involving a close friend's betrayal, left a deep scar on his heart and led him down a path of unforgiveness.

The betrayal by his friend had been a profound breach of trust, and Richard's anger and hurt ran deep. He couldn't fathom forgiving someone who had caused him so much pain. As time passed, Richard's resentment festered, and he became isolated from those around him.

Richard's unforgiveness became a heavy burden he carried with him every day. It affected his relationships with friends and family, as he struggled to trust anyone fully. The grudge he held had turned into a self-imposed prison of bitterness and isolation.

The story of Richard serves as a stark reminder of the corrosive nature of unforgiveness. It illustrates how holding onto grudges can lead to personal isolation and emotional turmoil. Richard's journey highlights the potential for personal growth when one chooses to break free from the suffocating grasp of unforgiveness.

The Choices We Make

The conclusion of these stories synthesizes the profound lessons gleaned from the narratives of forgiveness and unforgiveness. It emphasizes the transformative power of these choices in shaping our emotional well-being and relationships, underscoring the far-reaching consequences they can have on our lives. The stories of Mary, David, Sarah, Mark, Elena, and Richard collectively illustrate that forgiveness and unforgiveness are deeply personal journeys with profound effects. They serve as poignant reminders that the choices we make in the realm of forgiveness can either liberate our hearts and souls or imprison them in a cycle of pain and resentment.

Strategies for Forgiveness

- **Self-Compassion: The Foundation of Forgiveness**

Forgiveness often begins with self-compassion. This strategy encourages individuals to recognize and validate their own pain and emotions. By acknowledging one's suffering and offering self-compassion, it becomes easier to extend the same compassion to others.

The chapter delves into practices such as self-reflection and self-care that help individuals build a foundation of self-compassion. It emphasizes that forgiveness is not a sign of weakness but rather an act of strength that stems from a place of self-compassion.

- **Understanding the Offender's Perspective**

Empathy plays a crucial role in the forgiveness process. This strategy encourages individuals to try to understand the offender's perspective and motivations. It does not excuse the wrongdoing but rather provides insight into the complexity of human behavior.

The chapter explores techniques such as perspective-taking and open dialogue with the offender or a trusted mediator. It emphasizes that understanding the offender's perspective can be a powerful tool in fostering empathy and forgiveness.

❖ Emotional Processing: Navigating Pain and Anger

Processing and expressing emotions are an essential aspect of forgiveness. This strategy involves allowing oneself to feel and express the full range of emotions associated with the offense, including anger, sadness, and betrayal.

The chapter delves into methods such as journaling, therapy, and support groups that facilitate emotional processing. It emphasizes that acknowledging and processing these emotions is a crucial step toward forgiveness.

❖ Setting Boundaries: Protecting Yourself

Forgiveness does not require individuals to put themselves in harm's way or tolerate continued mistreatment. Setting boundaries is an essential strategy that allows individuals to protect themselves while still working toward forgiveness.

The chapter explores techniques for establishing healthy boundaries and maintaining them throughout the forgiveness process. It emphasizes that setting boundaries is an act of self-care and self-respect.

❖ Gradual Forgiveness: Step by Step

Forgiveness is not an all-or-nothing process; it can occur gradually. This strategy encourages individuals to take forgiveness one step at a time, acknowledging that it may not happen overnight.

The chapter outlines a step-by-step approach to forgiveness, allowing individuals to move at their own pace. It emphasizes that each small step toward forgiveness is a meaningful achievement.

❖ Release and Letting Go: The Act of Forgiveness

Ultimately, forgiveness involves releasing the emotional burden associated with the offense and letting go of the desire for revenge or retribution. This strategy explores techniques for actively practicing forgiveness, such as forgiveness letters or rituals.

The chapter delves into the power of forgiveness ceremonies and rituals in various cultures and belief systems. It emphasizes that forgiveness is a conscious choice that individuals can make to free themselves from the shackles of unforgiveness.

❖ Self-Forgiveness: Healing from Within

Forgiving oneself is often an overlooked aspect of forgiveness. This strategy encourages individuals to extend forgiveness to themselves for any perceived wrongs or mistakes they may have made in response to the offense.

The chapter explores methods for self-forgiveness, including self-compassion exercises and self-reflective practices. It emphasizes that self-forgiveness is a crucial component of the overall forgiveness journey.

❖ Maintaining Forgiveness: The Long-Term Commitment

Forgiveness is not a one-time event but an ongoing process. This strategy focuses on the importance of maintaining forgiveness and not letting resentment or bitterness creep back into one's life.

The chapter explores techniques for practicing forgiveness as a long-term commitment, including forgiveness reminders and gratitude practices. It emphasizes that maintaining forgiveness is a continuous effort that leads to lasting emotional freedom.

#Forgiveness HARVEST The Liberation of the Heart

Forgiveness and unforgiveness are powerful forces that shape our emotional landscapes and influence our journeys from adversity to flourishing. The act of forgiveness, though complex and challenging, holds the potential for profound personal growth, healing, and resilience. It is a testament to the human spirit's capacity to transcend pain and anger, choosing instead to embrace empathy, compassion, and ultimately, the liberation of the heart.

❖ **The Journey of Emotional Recovery:**

Navigating the Storm to Find Calm Waters

Emotional recovery is a multifaceted journey, marked by various stages and dimensions. Is a profound and often transformative journey that follows the turbulent seas of heartbreak, grief, loss, and forgiveness. This section will dip into the intricate nuances of this journey, highlighting its various stages and the resilience it instills in individuals as they strive to find calm waters amidst the emotional tempest.

Self-Compassion as a Lifeboat

At the heart of the journey of emotional recovery lies self-compassion—a critical lifeboat that keeps individuals afloat during tumultuous times. Self-compassion involves treating oneself with kindness, understanding, and patience, especially when grappling with grief, anger, or the complexities of forgiveness. It is the anchor that helps individuals weather the storm, preventing them from being consumed by self-blame or guilt.

The Role of Resilience

Resilience is both a guiding light and a destination on the journey of emotional recovery. As individuals navigate the choppy waters of heartbreak, they often discover reservoirs of resilience they may not have known existed. Resilience is not the absence of pain but the capacity to withstand and bounce back from it. It becomes a source of strength, providing the buoyancy needed to keep moving forward.

Rediscovering Purpose and Meaning

One of the challenges during emotional recovery is the sense of aimlessness that often accompanies heartbreak and grief. Individuals may feel adrift, as if their sense of purpose has been lost. Part of the journey involves rediscovering or redefining one's sense of purpose and meaning in life. This can be a deeply introspective process, leading to personal growth and transformation.

Trust as a Healing Anchor

In cases where trust has been eroded or shattered, whether due to betrayal or loss, the journey of emotional recovery often involves rebuilding trust. This process extends not only to others but also to oneself. It requires patience and discernment, as trust is gradually reconstructed, like a bridge over turbulent waters.

The Role of Support Systems

Navigating emotional recovery can be a challenging voyage, and support from friends, family, or support groups becomes essential. These supportive networks provide a safe harbor where individuals can share their experiences, express their emotions, and find solace in knowing they are not alone in their struggles.

Emotional Growth and Personal Transformation

Emotional recovery is not merely about returning to a previous state of emotional well-being but about undergoing profound growth and personal transformation.

It's about emerging from the journey with a greater sense of self-awareness, inner strength, and wisdom.

The Enduring Bonds of Resilience

Throughout the journey of emotional recovery, individuals often develop an enduring bond with resilience. It becomes a companion, a source of hope, and a reminder of their ability to overcome adversity. This bond extends beyond the journey itself, serving as a guiding star in navigating future challenges.

Real-Life Stories of Emotional Recovery:

Real-life stories abound with examples of individuals who have navigated the treacherous terrain of heartbreak and emerged on the other side.

Amy's Journey from Trauma to Triumph

Amy's life took a devastating turn when she became the victim of a traumatic event that left her emotionally scarred and struggling with crippling anxiety. The trauma she experienced seemed insurmountable, and for a long time, she felt trapped in a never-ending cycle of fear and despair.

In the aftermath of the trauma, Amy's life spiralled into chaos. She found herself unable to sleep, plagued by intrusive thoughts, and unable to engage in daily activities without crippling anxiety. It was a dark period in her life where happiness seemed like a distant memory.

However, Amy's journey toward emotional recovery began when she made the courageous decision to seek professional help. She started therapy, where she learned to confront the trauma and process her emotions. It was a difficult and painful process, but it was also a necessary step on her path to healing.

As time passed, Amy also leaned on the support of her loved ones. Their unwavering care and understanding played a crucial role in her recovery. Amy's journey was not without setbacks, but her determination to heal and her commitment to therapy allowed her to gradually regain control of her life.

Today, Amy is a beacon of resilience. While the trauma will always be a part of her story, she has learned to live with it and thrive despite it. Her journey serves as an inspiration to others who have experienced trauma, showing them that healing, and recovery are possible through vulnerability and seeking help.

Tom's Battle with Depression: A Journey from Darkness to Hope

Tom's life became a battleground when he found himself in the grip of depression. The darkness he felt was suffocating, and every day was a struggle to find even a glimmer of hope. His depression had become an all-consuming force that threatened to snuff out his zest for life.

Depression's grip on Tom was relentless. He experienced overwhelming sadness, a profound sense of hopelessness, and an overwhelming urge to isolate himself from the world. It felt like an uphill battle to simply get out of bed in the morning.

Tom's journey toward emotional recovery began when he reached out to a mental health professional. It was a difficult step, as depression often convinced him that seeking help was a sign of weakness. However, it was a step that ultimately saved his life.

Through therapy and, when necessary, medication, Tom began to slowly regain his sense of self. He learned to challenge the negative thought patterns that had kept him trapped in depression's clutches. Over time, he discovered that hope could be found even in the darkest of moments.

Today, Tom's life is a testament to the resilience of the human spirit. While depression will always be a part of his story, he has learned to manage it and find joy in life once again. His journey serves as a beacon of hope for others battling depression, showing that healing is possible when one chooses to confront their inner demons and seek help.

Maria's Healing Journey after Loss

Maria's world was shattered when she experienced a profound loss that left her heartbroken and struggling to make sense of her grief. The pain she felt was overwhelming, and she found herself adrift in a sea of sorrow.

In the days and weeks following her loss, Maria's emotions ranged from deep sadness to anger and confusion. She felt as though her world had been turned upside down, and the grief threatened to consume her.

Maria's journey toward emotional recovery began when she reached out to a grief support group. In the company of others who had experienced loss, she found solace in shared understanding and compassion. It was within this group that Maria learned that grieving was a natural and necessary process.

Over time, Maria's grief began to evolve. While the loss would always be a part of her story, she learned to carry it with grace and resilience. Maria's journey serves as a testament to the power of seeking support and allowing oneself to grieve. It illustrates that healing is possible, even in the face of profound loss.

Today, Maria honours the memory of her loved one by living a life filled with love and gratitude. Her journey offers solace and hope to others who have experienced loss, showing that emotional recovery is achievable through support, understanding, and the passage of time.

James' Path to Healing from Addiction

James found himself ensnared in the clutches of addiction, a relentless adversary that threatened to destroy his life. Substance abuse had become a way of coping with life's challenges, and it had led him down a dark and destructive path.

For James, addiction was a daily struggle. The substances he relied on had become a crutch that he believed he couldn't live without. The guilt and shame he felt about his addiction only fueled his cycle of substance abuse.

James' journey toward emotional recovery began when he decided to seek professional help. It was a decision marked by both fear and hope, as he knew that breaking free from addiction would be a daunting task. With the support of a therapist and a support group, he began the arduous process of recovery.

Through therapy, James learned to confront the underlying issues that had led to his addiction. He also discovered healthier ways of coping with life's challenges and stressors. The path to recovery was filled with ups and downs, but James remained committed to his journey.

Today, James lives a life free from the grip of addiction. While recovery is an ongoing process, he has learned to embrace a healthier and more fulfilling way of living. His story serves as a beacon of hope for others battling addiction, illustrating that healing is possible when one chooses to confront their addiction and seek support.

Emily's Resilience in the Face of Betrayal

Emily's life was upended when she discovered a profound betrayal by a close friend. The betrayal left her reeling, struggling to come to terms with the feelings of anger, hurt, and confusion that consumed her.

In the aftermath of the betrayal, Emily found herself grappling with a whirlwind of emotions. She was deeply hurt by the actions of her friend and struggled to understand why the betrayal had occurred.

Emily's journey toward emotional recovery began with a commitment to self-reflection and seeking therapy. She realized that holding onto anger and resentment was only causing her more pain. Through therapy, she learned to confront her emotions and find healthier ways of processing her feelings.

As time passed, Emily also found solace in rebuilding trust with friends who had always been there for her. She discovered the power of forgiveness as a means of liberating herself from the emotional burden of betrayal.

Today, Emily's life is marked by resilience and strength. While the betrayal will always be a part of her story, she has learned to rebuild trust and find joy in her relationships. Her journey serves as an inspiration to those who have faced betrayal, showing that emotional recovery is possible through self-awareness, vulnerability, and forgiveness.

David's Transformation After a Personal Crisis

David's life took a tumultuous turn when he faced a personal crisis that left him questioning his identity and purpose. It was a period of profound confusion, self-doubt, and existential despair.

During this crisis, David grappled with existential questions that had never surfaced before. He found himself adrift, searching for meaning and struggling to come to terms with the changes in his life.

David's journey toward emotional recovery began with a commitment to self-discovery and introspection. He sought guidance from therapists and embarked on a journey of self-exploration. Through this process, he began to piece together a new sense of self and purpose.

As David's self-discovery deepened, he also found strength in connecting with others who had faced similar crises. Support groups and shared experiences became invaluable sources of comfort and understanding.

Today, David's life is a testament to the power of introspection and self-awareness. He has learned to embrace the uncertainties of life and find meaning in the midst of change. His journey serves as an inspiration to those navigating personal crises, showing that emotional recovery is attainable through self-exploration and the courage to confront life's existential questions.

Conclusion: The Triumph of Emotional Recovery

The conclusion of these stories underscores the resilience and strength that individuals can find within themselves when they choose to confront adversity, embrace vulnerability, and embark on a journey toward emotional healing and resilience. These narratives serve as poignant reminders that emotional recovery is possible, even in the face of profound challenges, and that the human spirit has the capacity to triumph over adversity and find a path to healing.

Strategies for Emotional Recovery:

It's essential to dip into strategies and techniques to facilitate the process of emotional recovery. These strategies provide practical guidance for individuals seeking to navigate their journey from hardship and emotional distress to a state of flourishing and well-being.

Self-Care: Nurturing the Body and Mind

Self-care is a foundational strategy for emotional recovery. This section emphasizes the importance of prioritizing one's physical and mental well-being. It explores practices such as exercise, nutrition, sleep, and mindfulness that contribute to a sense of balance and vitality.

Readers are encouraged to cultivate self-awareness and listen to their bodies and minds. The chapter underscores that self-care is not selfish but a necessary act of self-compassion and self-preservation.

Embracing Resilience: Building Inner Strength

Resilience is a crucial component of emotional recovery. This strategy explores techniques for building inner strength and resilience, even in the face of adversity. It delves into the power of positive psychology, cognitive reframing, and affirmations.

Readers are encouraged to reframe their challenges as opportunities for growth and transformation. The chapter emphasizes that resilience can be cultivated and strengthened through intentional practices.

Seeking Support: Connecting with Others

Social support is a cornerstone of emotional recovery. This strategy emphasizes the importance of seeking support from friends, family, or support groups. It explores effective communication, active listening, and the power of vulnerability in forging meaningful connections.

Readers are encouraged to reach out to their support networks and share their feelings and experiences. The chapter underscores that seeking support is a sign of strength and resilience.

Mindfulness and Meditation: Cultivating Inner Peace

Mindfulness and meditation are powerful tools for emotional recovery. This section delves into mindfulness practices, meditation techniques, and deep breathing exercises that promote inner peace and emotional well-being.

Readers are guided through mindfulness exercises that help them stay present and reduce rumination. The chapter highlights that mindfulness fosters a sense of calm and clarity during challenging times.

Setting Goals and Taking Action: Regaining Control

Taking proactive steps toward one's goals is a key strategy for emotional recovery. This strategy explores the importance of setting achievable goals, creating action plans, and celebrating small victories along the way.

Readers are encouraged to regain a sense of agency and control over their lives. The chapter underscores that taking action, no matter how small, can empower individuals to move forward.

Creative Expression: Finding Healing Through Art

Creative expression can be a therapeutic outlet for emotional recovery. This section explores various forms of artistic expression, including journaling, painting, music, and writing, as tools for processing emotions and finding catharsis.

Readers are encouraged to explore their creative side and use art as a means of self-expression. The chapter highlights that creative expression can offer a sense of release and healing.

Forgiveness and Acceptance: Letting Go of Resentment

Forgiveness and acceptance are transformative strategies for emotional recovery. This strategy explores the power of forgiveness, both for others and oneself, in releasing emotional burdens and finding closure.

Readers are guided through forgiveness exercises and self-compassion practices. The chapter emphasizes that forgiveness is a choice that liberates individuals from the shackles of resentment.

Cultivating Gratitude: Focusing on the Positive

Gratitude is a mindset that can enhance emotional recovery. This section explores techniques for cultivating gratitude and shifting one's perspective toward the positive aspects of life.

Readers are encouraged to keep gratitude journals and practice gratitude rituals. The chapter underscores that gratitude can foster a sense of joy and contentment.

Seeking Professional Help: Guidance from Experts

Professional help is a valuable resource for emotional recovery. This strategy discusses the benefits of therapy, counseling, and psychiatric support. It provides guidance on how to find and connect with mental health professionals.

Readers are encouraged to prioritize their mental health and seek help when needed. The chapter emphasizes that professional guidance can provide tailored support on the path to emotional recovery.

Patience and Self-Compassion: Navigating the Journey

The journey of emotional recovery requires patience and self-compassion. This section explores the importance of being kind to oneself, acknowledging setbacks, and practicing self-forgiveness.

Readers are reminded that emotional recovery is not linear, and it's okay to have difficult days. The chapter underscores that self-compassion is a crucial ally on the journey toward well-being.

The Path to Emotional Flourishing

The conclusion of this section synthesizes the key strategies for emotional recovery and underscores their collective power in promoting emotional well-being and resilience. These strategies offer readers a roadmap for navigating their personal journey from adversity to emotional flourishing, highlighting that with commitment and intention, individuals can reclaim their sense of self and find renewed joy and fulfilment in life.

Chapter Six

Mental Health and Healing

Mental health is an integral component of the journey from adversity to flourishing. In chapter six, we explore the profound intersection between mental health and healing, delving into the complexities of the inner landscape and the transformative power of mental well-being.

The Inner Terrain of Mental Health

Mental health represents the inner terrain upon which the journey of healing unfolds. It encompasses the emotional, psychological, and cognitive aspects of an individual's well-being. Just as physical health is essential for a vibrant life, mental health plays a pivotal role in one's capacity to navigate and recover from adversity.

The Impact of Adversity on Mental Health

Adversity, in its various forms, can have a profound impact on mental health. Trauma, loss, and persistent stress can lead to conditions such as anxiety, depression, post-traumatic stress disorder (PTSD), and other mental health challenges. Understanding the connection between adversity and mental health is crucial in the process of healing.

The Stigma Surrounding Mental Health

Despite the growing awareness of mental health issues, stigma still surrounds the topic. Many individuals hesitate to seek help due to fear of judgment or societal misconceptions. Addressing this stigma is a critical step in promoting mental health as an integral aspect of healing.

The Importance of Self-Care

Self-care is foundational to mental health and healing. It involves practices and habits that support emotional and psychological well-being. Self-care may include mindfulness, meditation, physical activity, proper nutrition, and engaging in activities that bring joy and relaxation. It is a deliberate and ongoing commitment to nurturing one's mental health.

Seeking Professional Support

Just as physical health issues may require medical attention, mental health challenges often necessitate the support of mental health professionals. Therapists, counselors, and psychiatrists play vital roles in helping individuals navigate their mental health journeys. Seeking professional help is a sign of strength, not weakness.

The Role of Resilience in Mental Health

Resilience, a recurring theme in the journey of healing, is closely intertwined with mental health. Resilience involves the capacity to adapt and bounce back from adversity. Individuals with strong mental health often exhibit greater resilience, enabling them to better cope with life's challenges.

Breaking the Silence

Opening up conversations about mental health is a powerful step toward healing. Sharing one's experiences, challenges, and triumphs can reduce stigma, promote understanding, and create a supportive community. By breaking the silence surrounding mental health, individuals contribute to their own healing and that of others.

Strategies for Promoting Mental Health

Promoting mental health involves a holistic approach that addresses emotional, psychological, and cognitive well-being. Mental health is an integral component of overall well-being, and these strategies provide practical guidance for individuals seeking to nurture and safeguard their psychological and emotional well-being.

❖ **Self-Care as a Foundation**

Self-care is the cornerstone of mental health. This section emphasizes the importance of self-care practices such as regular exercise, balanced nutrition, adequate sleep, and stress management. Readers will learn how these fundamental practices contribute to mental wellness.

❖ **Mindfulness and Meditation**

Mindfulness and meditation techniques are powerful tools for promoting mental health. This strategy explores mindfulness practices that help individuals stay present, reduce stress, and enhance self-awareness. Readers will gain insights into the benefits of incorporating mindfulness into their daily routines.

❖ Emotional Regulation

Emotional regulation is a vital skill for mental well-being. This section delves into strategies for recognizing and managing emotions, including techniques for coping with stress, anxiety, and overwhelming feelings. Readers will learn how emotional regulation contributes to a balanced mental state.

❖ Building Resilience

Resilience is the ability to bounce back from adversity, and it plays a significant role in mental health. This strategy explores techniques for building resilience, including cognitive reframing, positive psychology, and adaptability. Readers will gain insights into how resilience can enhance their ability to navigate life's challenges.

❖ Social Connection and Support

Social connections are essential for mental health. This section emphasizes the importance of maintaining meaningful relationships, fostering social support networks, and seeking connection with others. Readers will learn how social bonds contribute to emotional well-being.

❖ Seeking Professional Help

Professional mental health support is a valuable resource. This strategy discusses the benefits of therapy, counseling, and psychiatric assistance. It provides guidance on how to find and connect with mental health professionals when needed. Readers will be encouraged to prioritize their mental health and seek help when necessary.

❖ Healthy Work-Life Balance

Balancing work and personal life is crucial for mental health. This section explores strategies for maintaining a healthy work-life balance, setting boundaries, and managing stress related to career and responsibilities. Readers will gain insights into creating a harmonious and fulfilling lifestyle.

❖ Creative Expression and Hobbies

Creative expression and engaging hobbies can foster mental well-being. This strategy delves into the therapeutic benefits of creative pursuits such as art, music, writing, and hobbies. Readers will learn how creative expression can provide an outlet for emotions and enhance mental clarity.

❖ Physical Activity

Physical activity is indeed a fundamental aspect of promoting and maintaining mental health. Regular exercise has been shown to have a positive impact on mental health by reducing symptoms of depression and anxiety. It encompasses a wide range of movements and exercises that benefit not only the body but also the mind. The connection between physical activity and mental health is deeply rooted in the mind-body relationship. Engaging in regular exercise triggers the release of various neurotransmitters and hormones in the brain. These neurochemicals play a crucial role in regulating mood, reducing stress, and promoting a sense of well-being.

❖ Gratitude and Positive Psychology

Cultivating gratitude and a positive mindset can contribute to mental health. This section explores techniques for practicing gratitude, embracing optimism, and focusing on positive aspects of life. Readers will gain insights into how a positive perspective can enhance emotional well-being.

❖ Coping with Change and Transitions

Change is an inevitable part of life, and coping with transitions is essential for mental health. This strategy discusses strategies for managing major life changes, adapting to new circumstances, and finding resilience during transitions. Readers will learn how to navigate change with a sense of purpose and resilience.

❖ A Holistic Approach to Mental Health:

The conclusion of this section synthesizes the key strategies for promoting mental health and emphasizes the importance of taking a holistic approach to mental well-being. These strategies offer readers a comprehensive framework for nurturing their psychological and emotional health, highlighting that with intention and practice, individuals can cultivate mental resilience, emotional balance, and a sense of fulfilment in their lives.

❖ The Healing Power of Mental Health

Chapter six explores the profound connection between mental health and healing. It emphasizes the importance of understanding and nurturing one's mental well-being as an integral part of the journey from adversity to flourishing. By recognizing the impact of adversity on mental health, breaking the silence surrounding mental health challenges, and embracing strategies for promoting mental well-being, individuals embark on a path of healing that encompasses not only their external circumstances but also the very core of their being—their mental health.

❖ Exploring Depression and Anxiety: Navigating the Shadows of the Mind

Depression and anxiety are two of the most prevalent and debilitating mental health conditions, often casting long shadows over the journey from adversity to healing. This exploration delves into the depths of depression and anxiety, shedding light on their complexities, impacts, and the paths to recovery.

The Complexity of Depression and Anxiety

Depression and anxiety are complex and multifaceted conditions, each with its own unique characteristics and manifestations:

Depression often presents as persistent feelings of sadness, hopelessness, and a lack of interest or pleasure in activities. It may be accompanied by physical symptoms such as changes in appetite and sleep patterns.

Anxiety encompasses a range of disorders, including generalized anxiety disorder, social anxiety disorder, and panic disorder. Common symptoms include excessive worry, restlessness, tension, and physical symptoms such as rapid heartbeat or trembling.

The Impact on the Journey of Healing

Depression and anxiety can cast long shadows over the journey of healing, affecting various aspects of an individual's life. Recovery from depression and anxiety is not always linear, and it may involve setbacks and relapses. However, with the right support and strategies, individuals can embark on a journey toward managing their symptoms, improving their overall well-being, and finding a sense of hope and purpose in their lives.

Emotional Impact

These conditions can intensify feelings of hopelessness, self-doubt, and despair, making it challenging to find motivation and meaning in the healing process.

Physical Well-being

Depression and anxiety can have physical manifestations, such as fatigue, sleep disturbances, and changes in appetite, further affecting one's overall well-being.

Interpersonal Relationships

The emotional toll of depression and anxiety can strain relationships with friends and family, potentially leading to isolation and loneliness.

Cognitive Functioning

Cognitive impairments, such as difficulties with concentration and decision-making, are common in depression and anxiety, making it challenging to engage fully in the healing journey.

Breaking the Silence

One of the most significant barriers to healing from depression and anxiety is the silence and stigma that often surround these conditions. Many individuals hesitate to seek help due to fear of judgment or misconceptions about mental health. Breaking the silence by opening up conversations about depression and anxiety is a powerful step toward healing and reducing stigma.

Seeking Professional Help

Professional help is a critical component of managing depression and anxiety. Mental health professionals, including therapists, counselors, and psychiatrists, can provide a range of treatments, including psychotherapy, medication, and coping strategies tailored to an individual's needs.

Coping Strategies

Coping with depression and anxiety involves developing a toolkit of strategies and practices to manage symptoms and promote well-being. These conditions can be challenging, but with a well-rounded approach, individuals can navigate the complexities of depression and anxiety more effectively. In this section, we will explore strategies and insights to further enhance your coping toolkit.

❖ Establishing a Daily Routine

Creating structure in your day can provide a sense of stability and purpose. Set daily routines that include regular mealtimes, exercise, work or study periods, and relaxation. Consistency in your schedule can help reduce feelings of unpredictability and chaos.

❖ Setting Boundaries

Establishing healthy boundaries is essential for managing stress and anxiety. Learn to say "no" when necessary, and prioritize self-care without guilt. Setting clear boundaries with work, social commitments, and personal relationships allows you to protect your mental and emotional well-being.

❖ Practicing Gratitude

Cultivating a gratitude practice can shift your focus from negativity to positivity. Each day, take a moment to reflect on what you're grateful for. This simple exercise can improve your overall outlook and enhance your ability to cope with difficult emotions.

❖ Avoiding Self-Isolation

While depression and anxiety may tempt you to isolate yourself, staying connected with others is crucial. Maintain social connections, even when it feels challenging. Sharing your feelings and experiences with trusted friends or support groups can provide emotional relief and perspective.

❖ Embracing Self-Compassion

Practice self-compassion by treating yourself with the same kindness and understanding you would offer to a friend. Recognize that experiencing depression and anxiety is not your fault, and it's okay to have difficult moments. Self-compassion can alleviate self-criticism and enhance your sense of self-worth.

❖ Engaging in Meaningful Activities

Participating in activities that bring you joy and fulfillment is essential. Whether it's a hobby, volunteering, or pursuing a passion, engaging in meaningful activities can boost your mood and sense of purpose.

❖ Identifying Triggers

Recognizing the triggers that exacerbate your symptoms is a crucial step. Keep a journal to track situations, thoughts, or events that worsen your depression or anxiety. Identifying triggers empowers you to take preventive measures and develop coping strategies.

❖ Developing Problem-Solving Skills

Enhance your problem-solving skills to address challenges more effectively. Break problems down into smaller, manageable steps, and brainstorm potential solutions. This proactive approach can reduce feelings of helplessness and increase your sense of control.

❖ Mindful Self-Compassion

Mindful self-compassion combines mindfulness and self-compassion practices. It involves being present with your emotions, acknowledging them without judgment, and responding with self-kindness. This technique fosters emotional regulation and resilience.

❖ Regular Check-Ins with Professionals

If you're receiving professional treatment, maintain regular check-ins with your therapist or psychiatrist. Open communication allows for adjustments in your treatment plan and ensures you're on the right path to recovery.

❖ Medication Adherence

If medication is part of your treatment plan, adhere to your prescribed regimen as directed by your healthcare provider. Medication can be a valuable tool in managing symptoms and stabilizing your mood.

❖ Celebrating Small Achievements

Acknowledge and celebrate your accomplishments, no matter how small they may seem. Overcoming depression and anxiety often involves taking incremental steps forward. Each achievement is a testament to your resilience and progress.

Building Resilience and Well-Being

In conclusion, coping with depression and anxiety is a journey of building resilience and well-being. Your toolkit is a collection of strategies and practices that empower you to navigate the challenges of these conditions. By incorporating these additional insights and continuously expanding your coping repertoire, you can cultivate the strength and resilience needed to overcome the obstacles on your path to recovery. Remember that seeking professional help and surrounding yourself with a supportive network are crucial components of your journey towards healing and emotional well-being.

Navigating the Shadows towards the Light

Depression and anxiety are shadows that can obscure the path of healing, but they are not insurmountable. By understanding the complexities of these conditions, breaking the silence surrounding them, seeking professional help, and embracing coping strategies, individuals can navigate the shadows toward the light of healing and well-being. With patience, resilience, and support, the journey from adversity to flourishing becomes an attainable and transformative voyage, even in the presence of depression and anxiety.

Real-Life Stories of Triumph

In this section, we will delve into real-life stories of individuals who have triumphed over depression and anxiety, shedding light on their personal journeys of recovery, resilience, and hope. These stories serve as beacons of inspiration, illustrating that healing is possible, and that through determination and support, individuals can overcome even the most challenging mental health struggles.

Sarah's Journey from Darkness to Radiance:

Sarah's life was once shrouded in the darkness of depression. She found herself trapped in a relentless cycle of sadness, hopelessness, and self-doubt. Every day was a struggle to find even a glimmer of light. However, Sarah's determination to regain her life led her to seek professional help.

With the support of a skilled therapist and the love of her family, Sarah embarked on a journey of self-discovery and healing. Through therapy, she learned to identify and challenge the negative thought patterns that had kept her captive for so long. Sarah also embraced mindfulness and meditation, which helped her find solace in the present moment.

Today, Sarah radiates resilience and vitality. While she acknowledges that depression will always be a part of her story, she has learned to manage it with grace and determination. Her story serves as an inspiration to others battling depression, reminding them that with the right support and self-care, healing is possible.

Mark's Triumph Over Debilitating Anxiety

Mark's life was dominated by debilitating anxiety that left him feeling trapped and overwhelmed. Simple tasks became daunting challenges, and social interactions were anxiety-inducing. His anxiety had a profound impact on his quality of life, but he was determined to break free from its grip.

Mark's journey to triumph began with therapy, where he learned coping strategies and techniques to manage his anxiety. Exposure therapy and cognitive-behavioral strategies helped him confront and gradually overcome his fears and triggers. He also cultivated mindfulness practices to ground himself during moments of panic.

Over time, Mark's world began to expand. He started to engage in social activities he once avoided and pursued his passions with renewed enthusiasm. Today, Mark lives a life free from the suffocating grip of anxiety. His story serves as a testament to the power of resilience and determination in the face of mental health challenges.

Jessica's Path to Emotional Recovery

Jessica's life took an unexpected turn when she experienced a traumatic event that left her struggling with both anxiety and depression. The weight of the trauma seemed insurmountable, and she felt like she was living in a constant state of fear.

Seeking help from a trauma-informed therapist was a pivotal moment in Jessica's journey. Through therapy, she learned to confront the trauma, process her emotions, and develop healthy coping mechanisms. Support from a close-knit group of friends and family provided her with the encouragement she needed.

With time and resilience, Jessica began to rebuild her life. She discovered a newfound strength and sense of purpose through volunteering and helping others who had experienced trauma. Jessica's story is a testament to the transformative power of therapy, support networks, and the human spirit's capacity for healing.

Alex's Journey of Resilience

Alex faced the daunting challenge of managing both depression and anxiety simultaneously. The weight of these conditions made every day feel like an uphill battle, and he often questioned whether he would ever find relief.

With the guidance of a skilled therapist, Alex began to untangle the complex web of his emotions and thought patterns. He learned techniques for managing both depression and anxiety, including cognitive-behavioral strategies and relaxation exercises. He also embraced physical fitness as a means of reducing symptoms and boosting his mood.

As time passed, Alex's resilience grew. He became an advocate for mental health awareness, sharing his story and supporting others on their journeys. Today, Alex lives a life marked by purpose and positivity. While depression and anxiety remain a part of his story, he has learned to manage them effectively and find joy in everyday life.

Triumphing Over Darkness

These real-life stories of triumph remind us that healing is attainable, and recovery is a dynamic and ongoing process. They illustrate that individuals can find their way out of the darkest of moments, navigate the complexities of depression and anxiety, and emerge stronger, more resilient, and full of hope. These stories serve as a testament to the strength of the human spirit and the transformative power of seeking help, resilience, and unwavering determination in the face of mental health challenges.

❖ **Seeking Help and Support:**

The Guiding Light in the Darkness

One of the most pivotal steps in the journey of healing from adversity, particularly when grappling with mental health challenges like depression and anxiety, is seeking help and support. This section explores the vital role that reaching out to others plays in the process of recovery.

Overcoming the Hurdles of Silence

The decision to seek help often begins with overcoming the barriers of silence and stigma that can shroud mental health issues. It is an act of courage to acknowledge one's struggles and to reach out for support, and it is essential to recognize this courage. Silence can perpetuate suffering, while reaching out can pave the way for healing.

The Healing Power of Connection

Human beings are inherently social creatures, and connection is a fundamental aspect of our well-being.

Depression and anxiety can lead to isolation and withdrawal, intensifying feelings of despair. Seeking help and support fosters connection—whether with friends, family, or mental health professionals—and can serve as a lifeline in times of darkness.

Friends and Family as Pillars of Strength

Friends and family often serve as the initial pillars of support in the journey of healing. Their understanding, empathy, and willingness to listen can provide a safe harbor during turbulent times. Sharing one's struggles with loved ones can be a profound step toward healing and can strengthen the bonds of trust and connection.

The Role of Mental Health Professionals

Mental health professionals, including therapists, counselors, psychiatrists, and psychologists, bring specialized knowledge and expertise to the journey of healing. They offer a structured and supportive environment for individuals to explore their thoughts, emotions, and experiences. Therapy provides tools and strategies for managing symptoms, addressing underlying issues, and fostering personal growth.

The Importance of Peer Support

Peer support, in the form of support groups or peer-led initiatives, offers a unique kind of understanding. Connecting with others who have walked a similar path can reduce feelings of isolation and provide valuable insights and coping strategies. Peer support emphasizes the notion that individuals are not alone in their struggles.

The Role of Medication and Treatment Plans

For some individuals, medication may be a crucial component of their treatment plan. Decisions about medication should be made collaboratively with healthcare providers, taking into account the individual's unique needs and preferences. Medication can alleviate symptoms and create a stable foundation for healing.

Building a Support Network

Creating a robust support network is akin to constructing a safety net during the journey of healing. It involves not only reaching out to friends, family, and professionals but also connecting with community resources, such as crisis hotlines or nonprofit organizations. Building a comprehensive support network ensures that individuals have access to help and guidance when needed.

Cultural Sensitivity and Diversity

Recognizing the diversity of experiences and cultural contexts is crucial in seeking help and support. Mental health professionals who prioritize cultural sensitivity and competence can offer more tailored and effective interventions. Individuals from various cultural backgrounds may face unique challenges and stigmas related to mental health, and culturally informed support can bridge these gaps.

Embracing Vulnerability and Honesty

Seeking help and support requires vulnerability and honesty. It involves the courage to share one's innermost thoughts and emotions, even when they may feel overwhelming or difficult to articulate. This vulnerability is a testament to inner strength and a catalyst for understanding and healing.

The Reciprocity of Support

While individuals seek help and support, it is also essential to recognize the reciprocal nature of these relationships. Just as one receives support, one can also offer support to others who may be facing similar challenges. This reciprocity reinforces the interconnectedness of humanity and the power of compassion.

Crafting a Tailored Support Network

Each individual's journey of healing is unique, and the support network should be tailored to their specific needs. This may involve a combination of professionals, friends, family, and community resources. Crafting this network is an ongoing process, adapting to the changing needs and phases of the healing journey.

The Transformative Power of Empathy

Empathy is the cornerstone of effective support. It is the capacity to understand and share the feelings of another. When individuals feel truly heard and understood, it can alleviate their sense of isolation and promote healing. Empathy fosters a sense of validation, reducing shame and self-blame.

Balancing Independence and Interdependence

The journey of healing involves a delicate balance between independence and interdependence. While seeking help and support is vital, it is equally important for individuals to cultivate their self-reliance and coping skills. Balancing these aspects empowers individuals to navigate future challenges with greater resilience and confidence.

Illuminating the Path Forward

In conclusion, seeking help and support is not a sign of weakness but a beacon of hope on the journey of healing. It is the recognition that no one should navigate adversity, depression, or anxiety alone. By breaking the silence, fostering connection, and embracing the many forms of support available, individuals can illuminate the path forward. Help and support are the guiding lights in the darkness, leading individuals from despair to the hope of healing and recovery.

❖ The Path to Mental Wellness:

Nurturing the Garden of the Mind

The journey toward mental wellness is a profound odyssey that encompasses self-discovery, healing, and the cultivation of inner resilience. This section explores the various elements and practices that compose the path to mental well-being.

Self-Exploration and Self-Awareness

The path to mental wellness begins with self-exploration and self-awareness. It involves a deep dive into one's thoughts, emotions, values, and beliefs. Self-awareness allows individuals to gain insight into their mental and emotional landscapes, fostering a more profound understanding of themselves.

Mindfulness and Present-Moment Awareness

Mindfulness is a cornerstone of mental wellness. It involves cultivating present-moment awareness without judgment. Mindfulness practices, such as meditation and mindful breathing, allow individuals to anchor themselves in the here and now, reducing anxiety about the future and regrets about the past.

Emotional Regulation and Coping Strategies

Developing emotional regulation skills and coping strategies is essential for managing the ups and downs of life. Techniques like emotional self-soothing, deep breathing, and grounding exercises enable individuals to navigate intense emotions more effectively.

Building Resilience Through Adversity

Resilience is the capacity to bounce back from adversity and adapt to challenges. Building resilience involves developing problem-solving skills, fostering a growth mindset, and strengthening one's ability to cope with stress. Resilience acts as a protective shield against the impact of adversity on mental wellness.

The Role of Positive Psychology

Positive psychology emphasizes the cultivation of positive emotions, strengths, and virtues as a means to enhance well-being. Practices like gratitude journaling, savoring positive experiences, and focusing on one's strengths can promote mental wellness.

Nurturing Healthy Relationships

Healthy relationships play a pivotal role in mental wellness. Cultivating supportive, authentic connections with others provides emotional nourishment and a sense of belonging. Effective communication, boundaries, and empathy are essential components of healthy relationships.

Self-Care and Holistic Well-Being

Self-care involves prioritizing one's physical, emotional, and psychological well-being. Engaging in regular exercise, maintaining a balanced diet, getting adequate sleep, and participating in activities that bring joy are crucial aspects of self-care. Holistic well-being encompasses all dimensions of health, creating a sense of harmony and balance.

Seeking Professional Guidance

When faced with complex mental health challenges, seeking professional guidance is a crucial step. Mental health professionals can provide tailored interventions, including therapy, medication, and treatment plans, to address specific issues and promote well-being.

Contributing to a Supportive Community

Active participation in a supportive community or social network is a powerful way to enhance mental wellness. Contributing to the well-being of others, volunteering, or engaging in group activities fosters a sense of purpose and connection.

Embracing Life's Seasons

Just as nature experiences seasons of growth, change, and renewal, so too does the journey to mental wellness. Individuals are encouraged to embrace these seasons, recognizing that they offer opportunities for learning, growth, and transformation. Adversity, setbacks, and challenges can serve as fertile ground for resilience and self-discovery.

The Art of Self-Compassion

Self-compassion is an essential tool in the garden of mental wellness. It involves treating oneself with kindness and understanding, particularly during times of difficulty or self-criticism. Self-compassion allows individuals to weather life's storms with greater resilience and self-acceptance.

The Role of Purpose and Meaning

A sense of purpose and meaning infuses life with vitality and resilience. Individuals are encouraged to explore their passions, values, and aspirations to discover what truly matters to them. Cultivating a sense of purpose can provide a guiding star during challenging times.

The Healing Power of Nature

Nature has a profound impact on mental well-being. Spending time in natural settings, whether it be a walk in the woods, a day at the beach, or simply tending to a garden, can soothe the mind, reduce stress, and foster a sense of peace and tranquillity.

Mindful Self-Reflection

Mindful self-reflection is a practice that allows individuals to gain deeper insight into their thoughts, emotions, and behaviors. Through journaling, meditation, or contemplative walks, individuals can explore their inner landscapes and gain clarity on their mental wellness journey.

The Ongoing Journey of Growth

The path to mental wellness is not a destination but an ongoing journey of growth and self-discovery. It is a commitment to continuous learning, adaptation, and self-compassion. Embracing the ebb and flow of life's challenges and joys is an integral part of this journey.

The Garden of Inner Well-Being

The path to mental wellness is like to nurturing a garden of inner well-being. It involves tending to the soil of self-awareness, planting the seeds of resilience and self-care, and cultivating the blossoms of positive emotions and healthy relationships. It is a lifelong journey that acknowledges the complexities of the human experience and the potential for growth and flourishing. In traversing this path, individuals embark on a transformative odyssey toward mental wellness, tending to the garden of their minds with care, compassion, and resilience.

Chapter Seven

Religion and Resilience

The Sacred Path to Inner Strength

This chapter delves into the profound relationship between religion and resilience on the journey from adversity to well-being. It explores how faith, spirituality, and religious practices can be sources of inner strength and fortitude during challenging times. In the sacred journey towards inner strength, we begin by unraveling the intricate threads that compose its very essence.

The Essence of Inner Strength

Inner strength is not merely a manifestation of physical might or unwavering resolve. It extends far beyond the tangible, encompassing the spiritual, emotional, and mental dimensions of our existence. At its core, inner strength is the unwavering belief in oneself and one's ability to weather life's storms with grace and resilience.

The Role of Religion

For many, religion serves as a wellspring of inner strength. It provides a framework of beliefs, values, and practices that offer solace, guidance, and purpose. In times of adversity, faith can be a source of profound strength, providing individuals with a sense of divine support and a higher purpose to endure challenges.

Stories of Resilience

Resilience, too, plays a pivotal role in shaping inner strength. Resilient individuals possess the ability to bounce back from setbacks, drawing from their inner reservoirs of determination and fortitude. Stories of resilience from diverse backgrounds and cultures inspire us, showcasing the unwavering human spirit's capacity to endure, adapt, and thrive in the face of adversity.

The Interplay of Faith and Resilience

In the tapestry of inner strength, faith, and resilience are intertwined like threads of the same fabric. Faith can bolster resilience, offering individuals a sense of hope and purpose even in their darkest hours. Conversely, resilience can strengthen faith, as the ability to persevere in the face of challenges can deepen one's spiritual connection.

As we embark on this exploration, we invite you to reflect on your own experiences, beliefs, and stories of resilience that have shaped your journey. Together, we will define inner strength in the context of religion and resilience, understanding how these elements intertwine to fortify our spirits along the sacred path.

❖ Spirituality as a Source of Strength: Nurturing the Soul's Resilience

In this chapter, we embark on a profound exploration of spirituality as an unyielding source of inner strength, drawing inspiration from real-life stories of individuals who have harnessed their spiritual beliefs and practices to cultivate resilience in the face of adversity.

The Essence of Spirituality

Spirituality transcends the confines of organized religion, inviting individuals to embark on deeply personal journeys of self-discovery and connection with the sacred. It encompasses a diverse array of beliefs, from belief to unbelief and everything in between. At its core, spirituality seeks to answer questions about the nature of existence, purpose, and the interconnectedness of all life.

Life Story: Meet Sarah, a woman who found solace in nature's beauty and interconnectedness. Through her daily hikes in the wilderness, she discovered a profound sense of spirituality that transcended religious dogma. The mountains, the rivers, and the trees became her sanctuary, offering solace and inspiration during her battle with a chronic illness.

A Source of Meaning and Purpose:

Spirituality provides a profound sense of meaning and purpose, acting as a guiding light during life's darkest moments. It helps individuals make sense of suffering, offering answers that resonate with the depths of their souls. This sense of purpose becomes a cornerstone of resilience, enabling individuals to endure adversity with unwavering determination.

Life Story: Mark, a retired teacher, faced profound loss when his spouse of 50 years passed away. Their shared spiritual beliefs provided solace and a sense of purpose. Mark channeled his grief into volunteering at a local hospice, offering companionship and solace to those facing their final moments. In this act of service, he found renewed meaning in life.

Spiritual Practices for Resilience

Spiritual practices, whether through meditation, prayer, mindfulness, or rituals, serve as potent tools for resilience. These practices create a bridge to the sacred, fostering inner peace, centeredness, and alignment with one's spiritual beliefs. In the midst of adversity, these practices offer a sanctuary of calm and equanimity.

Life Story: Maria, a single mother of three, navigated the challenges of her demanding job and family responsibilities by incorporating mindfulness into her daily routine. In moments of stress, she paused to focus on her breath and connect with her spiritual beliefs. This practice helped her find resilience and inner strength to face life's complexities.

The Sanctuary of Solitude

Solitude is often regarded as a sacred space for deep reflection and spiritual connection. It provides individuals with the opportunity to commune with their inner selves, explore their beliefs, and find solace amidst life's challenges. In moments of solitude, individuals often discover a profound sense of clarity and resilience.

Life Story: John, a combat veteran, grappled with post-traumatic stress disorder (PTSD) upon returning home from deployment. Seeking solace, he embarked on a solitary journey into the wilderness, where he spent months reflecting on his experiences and connecting with the natural world. This solitude became a transformative source of healing and resilience.

Transcending Ego and Embracing Compassion

Spirituality frequently encourages individuals to transcend the limitations of the ego and embrace compassion for themselves and others. This transformative shift reduces feelings of self-centeredness and promotes empathy, creating a reservoir of resilience rooted in compassion and interconnectedness.

Life Story: Emily, a survivor of a near-fatal car accident, underwent a profound spiritual awakening during her recovery. She found solace in forgiveness, not only for the driver who caused the accident but also for herself. Through this act of forgiveness, she discovered a wellspring of inner strength that propelled her toward recovery and advocacy for road safety.

The Interconnectedness of All Beings

Many spiritual traditions emphasize the interconnectedness of all beings and the recognition that suffering is a universal human experience. This perspective fosters a sense of unity and shared humanity, reinforcing the idea that no one is alone in their struggles. It becomes a source of resilience rooted in compassion and empathy.

Life Story: James, a man who battled addiction for years, found support and transformation in a spiritual recovery group. Through sharing his experiences and listening to others' stories, he realized the interconnectedness of their journeys. This realization fueled his commitment to sobriety and became a source of resilience in his ongoing recovery.

The Sacred Symphony of Spirituality and Resilience

In conclusion, in the depths of adversity, spirituality serves as a timeless wellspring of resilience. By exploring the essence of spirituality, embracing its practices, and connecting with like-minded souls, individuals embark on a profound journey toward healing and well-being. Real-life stories of Sarah, Mark, Maria, John, Emily, and James illuminate the transformative power of spirituality as they navigate their paths from adversity to inner strength and spiritual growth. These stories remind us that amidst life's challenges, spirituality becomes a sacred symphony, guiding individuals toward a place of profound resilience and healing.

As we journey together along the sacred path, may you find inspiration and guidance in the profound source of spirituality. May it empower you to harness your inner strength, embrace adversity as an opportunity for growth, and navigate life's complexities with a resilient and open heart.

I would like to share a further inspiring real-life story of a Christian individual who faced adversity, hardship, and loss, and managed to bounce back with faith and resilience:

Real-Life Story

Johnny Erickson Tada - Triumph Over Paralysis:

Johnny Erickson Tada's life journey is a profound testament to her unwavering Christian faith, resilience, and triumph over adversity.

Early Life and Tragic Accident

Johnny grew up in a Christian family and was an active, adventurous young woman.

At the age of 17, a diving accident in 1967 left her paralyzed from the neck down, completely altering the course of her life.

Dark Nights of the Soul

The accident plunged Johnny into deep despair and caused her to question her faith.

She struggled with depression, anger, and a sense of hopelessness as she grappled with the profound loss of her physical abilities.

Spiritual Resilience and Purpose

Johnny's Christian faith played a pivotal role in her recovery and resilience.

Through prayer, Bible study, and the support of her family, she found the strength to rebuild her life.

Creating a Ministry

Johnny founded Joni and Friends, an organization dedicated to providing support and resources for people with disabilities and their families.

Her story and ministry have inspired countless individuals worldwide.

Artist, Author, and Speaker

Despite her physical limitations, Johnny learned to paint by holding a brush between her teeth.

She has authored numerous books, including her autobiography "Joni," and is a sought-after speaker.

Legacy of Resilience and Faith

Johnny Erickson Tada's journey from the depths of despair to a life of purpose, advocacy, and faith-based ministry is a powerful example of spiritual resilience.

Her story reminds us that even in the face of life-altering adversity and hardship, faith and resilience can lead to a life of profound impact and purpose. Johnny Erickson Tada's life journey illustrates how one's Christian faith can serve as a source of resilience and hope during the darkest moments. Her ability to bounce back from a devastating accident and transform her life into a ministry of support, inspiration, and advocacy showcases the extraordinary power of faith, resilience, and unwavering determination.

Real-Life Story

Nick Vujicic - Rising Above Limitations:

Nick Vujicic, a Christian motivational speaker and author, was born in 1982 in Melbourne, Australia, with a rare condition known as tetra-amelia syndrome, which left him without limbs.

Early Challenges

Nick faced unimaginable physical challenges from birth, struggling to perform even the most basic tasks without arms and legs.

Growing up, he often felt isolated and experienced severe bouts of depression and loneliness.

A Spiritual Awakening

Despite his physical limitations, Nick's Christian faith became a source of strength and resilience.

He realized that his purpose in life was not defined by his physical condition but by his faith and determination.

Inspirational Speaker and Author

Nick Vujicic began speaking publicly at the age of 19, sharing his story of faith, hope, and resilience with audiences worldwide.

He founded the nonprofit organization Life Without Limbs to support and inspire people facing adversity.

International Impact

Nick's inspirational talks and books, such as "Life Without Limits" and "Unstoppable," have reached millions of people, encouraging them to overcome challenges, find purpose, and have faith.

He has travelled the world, meeting world leaders, and inspiring individuals from all walks of life.

Family and Advocacy:

Nick is a loving husband and father, demonstrating that a fulfilling family life is possible despite his physical condition.

He continues to advocate for people with disabilities, promoting acceptance and inclusion.

Legacy of Resilience and Faith

Nick Vujicic's life story is a powerful testament to the human spirit's ability to rise above adversity through faith and resilience.

His unwavering belief in God's plan for his life has allowed him to overcome physical limitations and inspire countless individuals to live with hope and purpose.

Nick Vujicic's journey from a life of physical challenges to becoming a renowned motivational speaker and author exemplifies the incredible strength of faith and resilience. His story serves as an enduring source of inspiration, reminding us that, with unwavering faith and determination, we can overcome even the most daunting obstacles and bounce back from adversity with grace and purpose.

❖ Finding Purpose and Meaning: The Resilient Quest for Life's Deeper Significance

In this deeper exploration of the profound quest for purpose and meaning, we delve into real-life stories that illustrate how individuals have unearthed purpose amidst adversity, underscoring the resilience that this journey fosters.

The Quest for Purpose

The human quest for purpose transcends circumstance and adversity. It is an intrinsic drive that compels individuals to seek deeper connections, meaning, and a sense of direction in their lives. This quest becomes a guiding light during the darkest moments.

Life Story: Julia, a survivor of domestic abuse, embarked on a mission to empower women who had experienced similar hardships. She founded a non-profit organization that provided resources, support, and counseling to survivors. Julia's journey from victim to advocate became her purpose, transforming her own pain into resilience.

The Unfolding Tapestry of Life

Life is akin to a tapestry, woven from countless threads representing unique experiences. Finding purpose involves stepping back to examine this tapestry in its entirety, recognizing how every thread, even the challenging ones, contributes to the intricate pattern of one's life.

Life Story: Carlos, who faced a debilitating injury that left him paralyzed, channeled his experience into motivational speaking. He shared his journey of adaptation and resilience with others, inspiring them to overcome their own obstacles. Carlos found purpose in helping others weave their threads of adversity into a tapestry of resilience.

Service and Contribution

Discovering purpose often unfolds through acts of service and contribution to others. These acts, whether big or small, can transform adversity into an opportunity to make a positive impact on the lives of others, infusing life with meaning and resilience.

Life Story: Emma, a cancer survivor, became deeply involved in fundraising for cancer research. She organized charity runs and events that raised substantial funds for cancer treatment and research. Emma's dedication to helping others battling the disease became her source of purpose and resilience.

Aligning with Values and Beliefs

Purpose frequently aligns with an individual's core values and beliefs. It involves living in harmony with deeply held principles, whether they are rooted in spirituality, ethics, or personal philosophy. This alignment infuses life with profound fulfillment and resilience.

Life Story: Daniel, a corporate executive, experienced a career burnout that prompted a reevaluation of his values. He transitioned into a non-profit organization focused on social justice, aligning his work with his strong ethical convictions. Daniel's newfound sense of purpose brought him fulfillment and resilience.

Legacy and Long-lasting Impact

Many individuals find purpose in the aspiration to leave a lasting legacy—a meaningful imprint on the world that endures beyond their lifetime. This pursuit of a significant legacy can inspire resilience as individuals work tirelessly to create something enduring.

Life Story: Rebecca, an educator, dedicated her life to improving education in underprivileged communities. She established scholarship programs and mentorship initiatives that transformed the futures of countless students. Rebecca's commitment to leaving a legacy of education became a source of purpose and resilience.

The Transformative Power of Meaning

The quest for purpose and meaning is transformative. It redirects focus from adversity to opportunity, from despair to hope. It bestows individuals with direction and a reason to persevere, even in the face of the most daunting challenges.

Life Story: Anthony, a survivor of a near-fatal accident, found his purpose in advocating for road safety and raising awareness about the consequences of reckless driving. His tireless efforts to prevent accidents and save lives became his mission, imbuing his life with profound meaning and resilience.

The Resilient Quest for Purpose and Meaning

In conclusion, the journey to discover purpose and meaning amid adversity is a testament to the indomitable human spirit. Real-life stories of Julia, Carlos, Emma, Daniel, Rebecca, and Anthony illuminate the transformative power of this quest. Their experiences remind us that amidst life's trials and tribulations, the search for purpose becomes a resilient journey—a quest that fuels hope, transforms despair, and guides individuals toward a brighter tomorrow.

❖ Navigating the Intersection of Faith and Resilience: A Journey of Strength and Belief

In this section, we embark on a profound exploration of how faith and resilience intersect in the face of life's trials and tribulations. We delve into real-life stories that exemplify the intricate dance between faith and resilience, revealing how individuals draw strength from their beliefs to overcome adversity.

The Dynamic Intersection of Faith and Resilience

Faith and resilience intersect at a dynamic crossroads, where deeply held beliefs provide the foundation for enduring adversity. This intersection becomes a sanctuary of strength, guiding individuals through life's challenges with unwavering belief in a brighter future.

Life Story: Meet Ahmed, an immigrant who faced discrimination and cultural alienation in a new country. His unwavering faith in the power of unity and compassion led him to establish an organization that promotes intercultural understanding and harmony. Ahmed's faith in humanity became the cornerstone of his resilience.

Faith as an Anchor During the Storm

Faith often serves as a steadfast anchor during life's storms, providing individuals with a sense of stability and hope, even in the face of profound adversity. It reminds them that they are not alone and that there is a greater purpose to their struggles.

Life Story: Sarah, a woman who battled a life-threatening illness, found solace and strength in her faith community. Their prayers and support became a source of resilience, enabling Sarah to endure grueling treatments and emerge stronger on the other side.

Spiritual Practices and Resilience

Spiritual practices, whether through prayer, meditation, or rituals, play a pivotal role in nurturing resilience. These practices foster a profound sense of inner peace, mindfulness, and connection with the divine, equipping individuals to confront adversity with grace.

Life Story: David, a man who faced financial ruin, turned to daily meditation and prayer to navigate the turbulent waters of uncertainty. Through these practices, he found the clarity and inner strength to make wise decisions and rebuild his life.

The Role of Faith Communities

Faith communities often serve as pillars of support and solidarity. They offer individuals a sense of belonging, emotional support, and a shared sense of purpose. In times of hardship, these communities become havens of comfort and guidance.

Life Story: Maria, a survivor of domestic abuse, found refuge and healing in her church community. They provided her with emotional support, counseling, and resources to rebuild her life. Maria's faith community became an essential part of her resilience journey.

Moral and Ethical Guidance

Religious and spiritual beliefs provide moral and ethical frameworks that guide individuals in making meaning out of adversity. These frameworks offer principles for living with integrity, compassion, and empathy, promoting inner resilience.

Life Story: Michael, a man who faced ethical dilemmas in his professional life, turned to his faith's teachings for guidance. His commitment to living in accordance with his beliefs not only helped him navigate challenging decisions but also reinforced his inner resilience.

Coping with Existential Questions

During times of adversity, individuals often grapple with existential questions about the nature of suffering, the meaning of life, and the concept of destiny. Faith and spirituality offer answers, solace, and a sense of purpose in the face of life's uncertainties.

Life Story: Emily, a survivor of a natural disaster that claimed her home and belongings, found solace in her spiritual beliefs. She viewed the disaster as an opportunity for rebirth and renewal, deepening her faith in the resilience of the human spirit.

The Intersection of Faith and Mental Health

Understanding the complex interplay between faith and mental health is crucial. While faith can be a source of resilience, it can also present challenges, such as religious guilt or conflicts between beliefs and mental health needs. Navigating this intersection requires sensitivity and balance.

Life Story: James, a man who struggled with depression, sought the support of a therapist who respected his religious beliefs. Through a combination of therapy and faith-based practices, he found healing and resilience.

The Intersection of Belief and Strength

To bring this section to a conclusion, the intersection of faith and resilience is a profound journey that enriches the human experience. Real-life stories of Ahmed, Sarah, David, Maria, Michael, Emily, and James illuminate the transformative power of this intersection. Their experiences remind us that amidst life's trials and tribulations, faith becomes a resilient journey—a journey that fortifies hope, nurtures strength, and guides individuals toward a brighter tomorrow.

Part Three

Chapter Eight

The Journey of Rejection: Navigating Life's Heartaches

In this chapter, we embark on a profound exploration of the intricate journey of rejection—a universal experience that often leaves scars on the human heart. Delving into the depths of real-life stories, we uncover how individuals confront rejection and emerge with newfound resilience, wisdom, and self-discovery.

The Heartache of Rejection

Rejection is a powerful emotional force, capable of shaking the very foundations of one's identity and self-worth. Whether in the realms of relationships, career, or personal aspirations, the sting of rejection can leave lasting imprints. This chapter explores the multifaceted dimensions of rejection and how individuals navigate its tumultuous waters.

Life Story: Meet Amy, a woman who experienced the heartache of a romantic rejection that shattered her dreams of a future together. Her journey through the labyrinth of emotions—pain, anger, self-doubt, and ultimately, acceptance—offers a poignant testament to the profound impact of rejection on one's emotional landscape.

The Anatomy of Rejection

Rejection is not merely an external event; it is an internal experience that prompts deep introspection and self-evaluation. We delve into the complex psychological and emotional responses to rejection, unraveling the layers of hurt, shame, and vulnerability it often brings to the surface.

Life Story: Hubert, a recent college graduate who faced numerous job rejections in a competitive job market, shares his emotional rollercoaster—initial optimism, the crushing weight of rejection emails, and the introspective journey that ultimately led him to reevaluate his career path.

Resilience in the Face of Rejection

This chapter illuminates the resilience that emerges when individuals confront rejection head-on. It explores the coping mechanisms, support systems, and personal growth that often accompany the experience of rejection, transforming it into an opportunity for self-discovery and renewal.

Life Story: Maria, an aspiring artist whose work was repeatedly rejected by galleries, found the courage to create a personal exhibition. Through her journey of self-expression and vulnerability, she not only overcame her fear of rejection but also discovered her unique artistic voice.

The Role of Self-Worth

Rejection has a profound impact on one's self-worth and self-esteem. This chapter delves into the ways individuals rebuild their self-worth after experiencing rejection, emphasizing the importance of self-compassion and self-acceptance in the healing process.

Life Story: Michael, a man who faced rejection in his personal relationships, embarked on a journey of self-discovery and self-love. His transformative process, marked by therapy and self-reflection, demonstrates how rebuilding self-worth can be a powerful act of resilience.

Turning Rejection into Fuel

Rejection can serve as a catalyst for growth and transformation. This chapter explores how individuals harness the pain of rejection as fuel for self-improvement, reevaluation of goals, and determination to prove their worth.

Life Story: Emily, a writer whose manuscript was repeatedly rejected by publishers, channeled her disappointment into self-publishing and building a dedicated readership. Her story exemplifies how rejection can ignite a fiery determination to achieve one's dreams.

Forgiving and Healing

Healing from rejection often involves the complex journey of forgiveness—forgiving others for their role in rejection and forgiving oneself for perceived shortcomings. This chapter delves into the transformative power of forgiveness in the context of rejection.

Life Story: James, a man who faced rejection and exclusion from a close-knit social group, embarked on a journey of forgiveness that led to both personal healing and reconciliation with his friends.

Embracing Rejection as a Catalyst for Resilience

The journey of rejection is a profound and universal aspect of the human experience. Real-life stories of Amy, Hubert, Maria, Michael, Emily, and James illuminate the transformative power of this journey. Their experiences remind us that amidst the pain and heartache, rejection becomes a resilient journey—a journey that shapes character, nurtures growth, and ultimately guides individuals toward a deeper understanding of themselves and the world around them.

❖ Coping with Rejection and Abandonment: Embracing Healing and Self-Discovery

Coping with rejection and abandonment, are two deeply human experiences that can shake the very core of one's self-worth and emotional well-being. Drawing from real-life stories, we explore how individuals navigate the turbulent waters of rejection and abandonment, ultimately emerging with resilience, self-discovery, and newfound strength.

The Painful Echoes of Rejection and Abandonment

Rejection and abandonment are emotional earthquakes that can leave lasting tremors in one's life. This chapter begins by delving into the profound emotional impact of these experiences, recognizing the depth of the pain, vulnerability, and self-doubt they can elicit.

Life Story: Meet Yola, who grappled with the abandonment of a loved one during her childhood. Her journey through the layers of grief, anger, and the longing for closure unveils the profound impact of early abandonment on her adult life.

The Overlapping Terrain of Rejection and Abandonment

Between rejection and abandonment, recognizing that these experiences often intertwine, compounding the emotional turmoil. We explore the nuanced ways in which individuals cope with the convergence of these powerful emotions.

Life Story: Matt, a survivor of a tumultuous relationship that ended in abandonment, shares his journey of unraveling the intertwined threads of rejection and abandonment. His story illuminates the complexity of healing from overlapping emotional wounds.

Resilience in the Face of Emotional Turbulence

Coping with rejection and abandonment demands profound resilience. This section explores the coping mechanisms, support systems, and self-reflective processes that individuals employ to navigate emotional turbulence. It highlights the resilience that can emerge from the crucible of pain.

Life Story: Sue, who faced rejection and abandonment in her personal relationships, embarked on a journey of self-discovery and self-love. Her transformative process, marked by therapy and inner exploration, exemplifies how resilience can be nurtured in the face of emotional turmoil.

Rebuilding Self-Worth and Self-Compassion

One of the central challenges in coping with rejection and abandonment is the erosion of self-worth and self-compassion. This chapter delves into the ways individuals rebuild their sense of self-worth and cultivate self-compassion as they emerge from the depths of emotional pain.

Life Story: Femi, who experienced rejection in both his personal and professional life, found solace in the embrace of self-compassion. His journey toward self-worth and self-acceptance demonstrates the transformative power of self-compassion in healing.

From Victimhood to Empowerment

Coping with rejection and abandonment often involves a shift from feeling like a victim of circumstances to becoming an empowered survivor. Emily story's explores how she harnesses her pain as a catalyst for personal growth, empowerment, and transformation.

Life Story: Temi, who confronted rejection and abandonment in her personal and creative endeavors, channeled her pain into creative expression and self-discovery. Her story exemplifies how embracing empowerment can be a powerful response to emotional adversity.

Forgiveness and Healing

Forgiveness plays an essential role in the journey of coping with rejection and abandonment. Lusaco story's delves into the intricate process of forgiveness—forgiving others for their role in rejection and abandonment, and forgiving oneself for perceived shortcomings.

Life Story: Lusaco, who faced rejection and abandonment from a close-knit social group, embarked on a journey of forgiveness that led to both personal healing and reconciliation with his friends.

Embracing Healing and Self-Discovery

Coping with rejection and abandonment is a profound and often tumultuous journey that shapes one's character, resilience, and understanding of self and others. Real-life stories of Yola, Matt, Sue, Femi, Temi, and Lusako illuminate the transformative power of this journey. Their experiences remind us that amidst the pain and vulnerability, coping with rejection and abandonment becomes a resilient journey—a journey that ultimately guides individuals toward healing, self-discovery, and a deeper connection with their own inner strength.

❖ **Building Self-Esteem and Self-Worth: Reclaiming Your Inner Value**

Self-esteem and self-worth are the foundational building blocks of a fulfilling and resilient life. When individuals possess a healthy sense of self-esteem and self-worth, they are better equipped to navigate life's challenges, bounce back from setbacks, and pursue their dreams with confidence. In this chapter, we will explore the vital importance of nurturing and reclaiming one's inner value, using real-life stories that exemplify the transformative power of self-esteem and self-worth.

The Journey to Self-Acceptance:

Many individuals grapple with self-doubt and a lack of self-worth at various points in their lives. It is often a journey filled with personal struggles and external pressures that can erode one's sense of self. However, as we delve into the following real-life stories, we will witness how individuals confronted their insecurities, reclaimed their inner worth, and emerged stronger and more self-assured.

The Power of Resilience and Self-Belief:

Real-life stories in this chapter will illustrate how individuals faced adversity, including bullying, societal expectations, and personal setbacks, and discovered the resilience within themselves to rebuild their self-esteem. They learned to appreciate their unique qualities and recognize their inherent worth.

Cultivating Self-Compassion:

Self-esteem and self-worth often go hand in hand with self-compassion. In this chapter, we will explore how individuals overcame their harshest self-critiques and embraced self-compassion as a tool for building a healthier self-image.

Embracing Imperfection and Authenticity:

The real-life stories featured here will showcase how individuals broke free from the pursuit of perfectionism and societal ideals, embracing their imperfections as part of their authentic selves. They found that their flaws and vulnerabilities were not weaknesses but strengths that contributed to their uniqueness.

Achieving Personal Growth and Fulfillment:

Ultimately, the journey to building self-esteem and self-worth is a path toward personal growth and fulfillment. These real-life stories will illustrate how individuals, through their self-discovery and inner transformation, achieved greater satisfaction in their relationships, careers, and overall well-being.

As we explore these stories of individuals who reclaimed their inner value, we will gain insights into the profound impact that self-esteem and self-worth can have on one's life. These stories will serve as beacons of inspiration, encouraging us to embark on our own journeys of self-discovery, self-acceptance, and personal growth.

Real-Life Story

Let's delve into a real-life story that exemplifies the theme of building self-esteem and self-worth:

Megan's Journey to Self-Discovery and Empowerment:

Megan's story is a testament to the transformative power of self-esteem and self-worth, illustrating how she overcame personal challenges to reclaim her inner value and live a life of empowerment.

Early Struggles:

- *Megan grew up in a family where academic achievement was highly emphasized. She felt immense pressure to excel in school and achieve perfection in every aspect of her life.*
- *Despite her efforts, she often received criticism and comparisons to her siblings, which eroded her self-esteem.*

Bullying and Peer Pressure:

- *In high school, Megan became a target of bullying due to her quiet and introverted nature. The relentless taunts and ostracization left her feeling isolated and worthless.*
- *She succumbed to peer pressure, attempting to fit in by adopting behaviors that went against her values.*

The Turning Point:

- *Megan reached a breaking point when she realized that seeking validation from others and conforming to societal expectations were detrimental to her well-being.*

- She embarked on a journey of self-discovery, seeking therapy and support to confront her insecurities and rebuild her self-esteem.

Embracing Authenticity:

- Through therapy, Megan learned to embrace her authentic self. She recognized her unique qualities and appreciated her introverted nature as a source of strength, enabling her to empathize deeply with others.
- She started setting boundaries with toxic individuals and distanced herself from negative influences.

Personal Growth and Empowerment:

- As Megan's self-esteem grew, she pursued her passion for art, eventually establishing a successful career as an artist.
- She became an advocate for mental health and self-acceptance, sharing her journey with others to inspire them to embrace their worth.

Impact on Others:

- Megan's story resonated with countless individuals who faced similar struggles. Her openness and vulnerability created a supportive community of people striving to build their self-esteem and self-worth.

Megan's journey reflects the profound transformation that is possible when one commits to reclaiming their inner value. Through self-discovery, self-acceptance, and the courage to embrace authenticity, she not only rebuilt her self-esteem but also empowered others to do the same. Her story serves as a reminder that self-worth is not defined by external validation but by the strength and authenticity that lie within us.

Real-Life Story

Here's another real-life story that highlights the journey of building self-esteem and self-worth:

David's Triumph Over Self-Doubt:

David's story is a powerful testament to the resilience of the human spirit and the capacity to overcome self-doubt to reclaim one's inner worth.

Early Struggles:

David grew up in a household where academic success was highly emphasized. As the youngest of three siblings, he often felt the pressure to live up to the high expectations set by his parents and siblings.

He struggled with feelings of inadequacy and constantly compared himself to his accomplished family members.

Academic and Personal Challenges:

Throughout school, David faced difficulties in keeping up with the rigorous academic standards he believed were expected of him.

His self-esteem plummeted as he received lower grades than he had hoped for and faced moments of public humiliation in class.

A Turning Point:

It wasn't until college that David began to question the relentless pursuit of external validation and perfectionism.

He sought therapy to address his self-doubt and began to explore his own passions and interests outside the rigid expectations of his family.

Embracing Imperfection:

Through therapy and self-reflection, David learned to embrace his imperfections as part of his unique identity. He realized that self-worth was not contingent on constant success but on self-acceptance and self-compassion.

He surrounded himself with supportive friends and mentors who encouraged his personal growth.

Bouncing Back and Thriving:

With renewed self-esteem and self-worth, David pursued a career that aligned with his true passions.

He became an advocate for mental health and perfectionism, sharing his journey and encouraging others to break free from the shackles of self-doubt.

Empowering Others:

David's story resonated with students and young adults facing similar pressures and self-doubt. He started mentoring programs and workshops to help others navigate the challenges of self-esteem and self-worth.

David's journey showcases the profound transformation that can occur when one confronts self-doubt and embraces their inherent worth. By letting go of external expectations and perfectionism, he discovered that self-esteem and self-worth are rooted in self-acceptance and authenticity. His story serves as a source of inspiration for individuals striving to overcome self-doubt and reclaim their inner value.

❖ Finding Acceptance Within Ourselves: Embracing Inner Peace and Self-Love

Finding acceptance within ourselves is often a profound and transformative journey that leads to inner peace and self-love. It involves embracing our flaws, acknowledging our past mistakes, and realizing that self-worth is not contingent on external validation. In this chapter, we will explore the concept of finding acceptance within ourselves through a real-life story that exemplifies the path to self-love and inner peace.

Real-Life Story

Emma's Journey to Self-Acceptance:

Emma's story is a poignant example of a person who embarked on a transformative journey to find acceptance within herself and, in doing so, discovered inner peace and self-love.

Early Struggles

Emma grew up in a society that often equated self-worth with appearance and material success. She adopted these values from a young age.

Throughout her teenage years and early adulthood, she constantly compared herself to others and felt a deep sense of inadequacy.

Perfectionism and External Validation

Emma sought validation through academic achievements, professional success, and the approval of others.

Despite her accomplishments, she remained plagued by self-doubt and a constant need for external validation.

The Awakening

It wasn't until a significant life event—a major career setback and the end of a long-term relationship—that Emma began to question her pursuit of external validation.

She realized that her relentless pursuit of perfectionism and external approval had left her feeling empty and unfulfilled.

The Path to Self-Acceptance:

Emma embarked on a journey of self-discovery, seeking therapy and practicing mindfulness and self-compassion.

She learned to embrace her imperfections, forgive herself for past mistakes, and cultivate self-love.

Inner Peace and Self-Love:

As Emma's journey unfolded, she found a sense of inner peace that transcended external circumstances.

She realized that self-acceptance was the key to self-love and that her worthiness was innate, irrespective of her achievements.

Impact on Others

Emma's transformation and newfound self-acceptance inspired those around her. She became an advocate for self-love and mental well-being, sharing her journey to encourage others.

Emma's story illustrates that finding acceptance within ourselves is a journey of self-discovery, self-compassion, and self-love. It highlights the profound impact that self-acceptance can have on one's overall well-being, leading to inner peace and a deep sense of fulfillment. Emma's journey serves as a beacon of hope for anyone seeking to break free from the chains of self-doubt and external validation and to find true acceptance within themselves.

Chapter Nine

Writing a Daring New Ending

let's dive into the concept of writing a daring new ending: The Power of Self-Transformation. Writing a daring new ending to our life story is a courageous act of self-transformation. It signifies our ability to break free from the constraints of past narratives, redefine our identity, and craft a future filled with purpose and authenticity. In this chapter, we will explore the concept of rewriting our life's narrative through a real-life story that exemplifies the transformative journey of self-reinvention and the power of embracing a daring new ending.

Real-Lift Story

Sarah's Journey of Self-Reinvention:

Sarah's story is a compelling example of an individual who embarked on a journey to rewrite her life's narrative, breaking free from the limitations of her past to embrace a daring new ending.

Past Limitations:

- Sarah had spent most of her life conforming to the expectations of her family and society. She pursued a career that was socially prestigious but unfulfilling to her.

- She had always dreamed of becoming an artist, but her fear of judgment and failure held her back.

Awakening to Authenticity:

- A significant life event—a health scare that prompted her to reevaluate her priorities—became the catalyst for her transformation.
- Sarah realized that life was too short to continue living a life that didn't align with her true passions and values.

Embracing Creativity:

- With newfound determination, Sarah decided to pursue her passion for art. She enrolled in art classes and began to create with unbridled enthusiasm.
- Despite initial self-doubt and challenges, she found immense joy in the process of self-expression.

Defying Expectations:

- Sarah's decision to pursue her artistic calling defied the expectations of her family and society. She faced criticism and skepticism from some.
- However, her inner conviction and newfound self-esteem allowed her to persevere.

Crafting a Daring New Ending:

- Over time, Sarah's dedication and talent led to recognition in the art world. She held her first solo exhibition, a testament to her journey of self-reinvention.
- Her daring new ending was not just about a career change but about embracing her authentic self and living life on her terms.

Inspiration for Others:

- Sarah's story inspired others to examine their own lives and question whether they were living authentically.
- She became an advocate for self-reinvention, sharing her journey to encourage others to pursue their passions and rewrite their life narratives.

Sarah's journey demonstrates the remarkable power of self-reinvention and the courage to embrace a daring new ending. It reminds us that we have the agency to transform our lives, break free from societal expectations, and create a future that resonates with our true selves. Her story encourages us to reflect on our own narratives and consider the bold steps we can take to rewrite our life's ending, turning it into a narrative of authenticity, fulfilment, and self-discovery.

The Catalyst for Change

Writing a daring new ending to one's life story often begins with a catalyst for change. This catalyst can be a significant life event, a moment of clarity, or a deep sense of dissatisfaction with the current narrative. In Sarah's case, it was a health scare that forced her to confront the reality of her life choices and question whether she was truly living in alignment with her values and passions. Such catalysts awaken a sense of urgency and a desire for personal transformation.

Confronting Fear and Self-Doubt:

Embracing a daring new ending requires confronting fear and self-doubt. When individuals decide to break free from the constraints of their past narratives, they often encounter internal resistance. Sarah, for example, had to grapple with the fear of judgment, failure, and the uncertainty of pursuing her passion for art. Overcoming these internal barriers is a critical step in the journey of self-transformation.

Discovering Authenticity

At the heart of rewriting one's life narrative is the discovery of authenticity. This involves peeling away the layers of societal expectations, external pressures, and self-imposed limitations to uncover one's true self. Sarah's decision to pursue her passion for art was not just a career change; it was an act of self-discovery. Through the process of creating art, she tapped into her authentic self and found a source of profound joy and fulfillment.

Resilience and Perseverance

The path to a daring new ending is rarely smooth. It is often marked by setbacks, challenges, and moments of doubt. Sarah faced criticism and skepticism from those who questioned her unconventional choice. However, her resilience and determination propelled her forward. Her ability to persevere in the face of adversity is a testament to the power of self-transformation.

Impact on Others

One of the remarkable aspects of rewriting one's life narrative is its ripple effect. Sarah's decision to embrace her authentic self and pursue her passion not only transformed her life but also inspired others. Her story became a source of motivation for individuals who had been living in conformity with societal expectations. It highlights the potential for personal transformation to inspire and uplift those around us.

Crafting a Legacy of Authenticity

Ultimately, the act of writing a daring new ending is about crafting a legacy of authenticity. It is about leaving behind a narrative that reflects one's true self, values, and passions. Sarah's daring new ending was not just a personal victory; it was a testament to the importance of living an authentic life. It serves as a source of inspiration for individuals who may be on the cusp of their own transformations.

In my own opinion, writing a daring new ending is the Power of Self-Transformation. It is a journey that begins with a catalyst for change, requires the courage to confront fear and self-doubt, leads to the discovery of authenticity, demands resilience and perseverance, and has the potential to inspire others. It is a reminder that we have the agency to rewrite our life's narrative and shape a future filled with purpose, authenticity, and self-discovery.

❖ Setting Goals for Personal Transformation: The Blueprint for Change

Setting goals for personal transformation is the foundational step in the journey of self-improvement and growth. It provides a clear direction, a sense of purpose, and a roadmap for individuals seeking to rewrite their life narratives and embrace a daring new ending. In this chapter, we will delve into the process of setting transformative goals, highlighting their significance through real-life examples of individuals who embarked on a path of profound change.

The Importance of Goal Setting

Goal setting serves as the compass that guides personal transformation. It helps individuals define their aspirations, break down their journey into manageable steps, and measure their progress along the way. Without clear goals, the path to self-transformation can feel aimless and overwhelming.

Identifying Your True Desires

One of the first steps in setting transformative goals is to identify one's true desires and values. This involves deep self-reflection and introspection. It requires individuals to ask themselves what they truly want in life, what brings them joy and fulfillment, and what aligns with their authentic selves.

SMART Goals:

Effective goal setting often follows the SMART criteria:

- Specific: Goals should be clearly defined and specific, leaving no room for ambiguity.
- Measurable: Goals should include measurable criteria to track progress.
- Achievable: Goals should be realistic and attainable, considering one's current circumstances.
- Relevant: Goals should align with one's values and aspirations, contributing to personal growth.
- Time-Bound: Goals should have a set timeframe for completion.

Real-Life Examples:

- *Sarah's Artistic Pursuit:* Sarah's transformative goal was to become a professional artist. Her SMART goal included enrolling in art classes, creating a portfolio, and participating in local art exhibitions within a specified timeframe.

- *David's Fitness Journey:* David's goal was to achieve better physical and mental health. He set SMART goals for regular exercise, dietary changes, and mindfulness practices. He also tracked his progress by measuring his fitness levels and emotional well-being over time.

- *Emma's Self-Love Commitment:* Emma's goal was to cultivate self-love and acceptance. She set daily, weekly, and monthly goals for self-compassion exercises, journaling, and self-affirmations. She measured her progress by tracking her emotional well-being and self-esteem.

Overcoming Challenges

The journey of personal transformation is not without its challenges. Individuals may encounter setbacks, face self-doubt, or struggle with motivation along the way. However, setting transformative goals provides a structured framework for overcoming these challenges. It allows individuals to break their journey into manageable steps and celebrate their achievements, no matter how small.

Adapting and Evolving

As individuals progress on their transformative journeys, they may find that their goals evolve and change. This is a natural part of growth. It's essential to remain flexible and open to adapting goals as circumstances and priorities shift.

Inspiring Others

Setting and achieving transformative goals can inspire and motivate others. When individuals witness the tangible results of personal transformation, it encourages those around them to embark on their own journeys of self-improvement and growth.

In inference, setting goals for personal transformation is the blueprint for change, providing direction, purpose, and a framework for self-improvement. By identifying true desires, following the SMART criteria, and persevering through challenges, individuals can rewrite their life narratives and craft a daring new ending. Through real-life examples, we see that transformative goals are not only achievable but also inspiring, offering a beacon of hope for anyone seeking positive change in their lives.

Whether you're striving for self-improvement, professional success, or any other aspect of your life, setting clear and meaningful goals provides a roadmap for your journey.

Here's a step-by-step guide on how to set and achieve your goals:

Self-Reflection and Clarity

- ❖ Begin by reflecting on your values, passions, and aspirations. What is truly important to you? What do you want to achieve in different areas of your life (e.g., career, relationships, health)?
- ❖ Define your long-term vision. Where do you see yourself in 1 year, 5 years, or even 10 years? Having a clear vision helps you set goals that align with your ultimate objectives.

Set Specific Goals

- ❖ Ensure that your goals are specific and well-defined. Vague goals are challenging to measure and work toward.

❖ Use the SMART criteria to make your goals Specific, Measurable, Achievable, Relevant, and Time-bound. For example, instead of saying, "I want to be healthier," you could say, "I will exercise for 30 minutes five days a week and reduce my sugar intake to one dessert per week for the next three months."

Prioritize Your Goals

❖ Determine which goals are most important to you. It's often helpful to focus on a few key objectives at a time to avoid feeling overwhelmed.

❖ Consider the short-term and long-term significance of each goal when prioritizing.

Break Down Larger Goals

❖ If you have big, long-term goals, break them down into smaller, more manageable steps. This makes it easier to track your progress and stay motivated.

❖ Create a timeline with milestones or checkpoints to assess your advancement.

Write Down Your Goals

❖ Put your goals in writing. This makes them more tangible and increases your commitment to achieving them.

❖ Consider keeping a journal or using goal-setting apps to track your progress.

Stay Accountable

❖ Share your goals with a trusted friend, family member, or mentor who can hold you accountable and provide support.

- ❖ Consider joining a group or community with similar goals, such as a fitness class or professional organization.

Take Action

- ❖ Taking action is the most crucial step in achieving your goals. Break your goals into daily, weekly, or monthly tasks, and start working toward them immediately.
- ❖ Stay disciplined and consistent in your efforts.

Measure Progress

- ❖ Regularly evaluate your progress by comparing it to the milestones you've set. Celebrate your achievements, no matter how small.
- ❖ If you encounter obstacles or setbacks, adjust your approach, but don't abandon your goals.

Stay Flexible

- ❖ Life is unpredictable, and circumstances can change. Be open to adjusting your goals as needed to accommodate new opportunities or challenges.

Seek Support and Resources

- ❖ Don't hesitate to seek guidance, resources, or education that can help you achieve your goals more effectively.
- ❖ Consider investing in courses, books, or workshops related to your goals.

Maintain Motivation

- ❖ Keep your motivation high by regularly reminding yourself of the reasons behind your goals and the benefits you'll gain from achieving them.

❖ Visualize your success and stay focused on the positive outcomes.

Review and Adjust

❖ Periodically review your goals and assess your progress. Celebrate your successes and make necessary adjustments to your action plan.

Remember that personal transformation is a journey, and setbacks may occur. However, with determination, focus, and a well-defined goal-setting process, you can make significant progress toward realizing your aspirations and rewriting your life's narrative.

❖ **Taking Inspired Action**

Taking inspired action is a powerful approach to achieving your goals and creating positive changes in your life. It involves aligning your actions with your inner inspiration, passion, and purpose.

Here's a guide on how to take inspired action:

1. Clarify Your Vision:

- Begin by gaining clarity on what truly inspires you. What are your passions, values, and long-term goals? Having a clear vision will help you identify the actions that resonate with your inner desires.

2. Connect with Your Why:

- Understand the deeper reasons behind your goals. Ask yourself why achieving a particular goal is meaningful to you. Connecting with your "why" provides motivation and inspiration.

3. Set Meaningful Goals:
- Ensure your goals are aligned with your values and aspirations. When your goals have personal significance, you're more likely to take inspired action to achieve them.

4. Listen to Your Intuition:
- Pay attention to your intuition and inner guidance. Sometimes, your gut feeling or inner wisdom can lead you toward the actions that are right for you.

5. Cultivate Mindfulness:
- Practice mindfulness to stay present and aware. Mindfulness can help you tap into your inner inspiration by quieting the noise of external distractions and worries.

6. Take Inspired Action Steps:
- When you feel a strong sense of inspiration or excitement about a particular action, seize that moment and take that step. Inspired actions often come with a sense of flow and energy.

7. Trust Your Instincts:
- Trust yourself and your instincts. Believe that you have the wisdom and intuition to make choices that align with your higher purpose.

8. Embrace Fear and Doubt:
- It's natural to experience fear and doubt when taking bold actions. Acknowledge these feelings, but don't let them paralyze you. Use

them as indicators that you're stepping out of your comfort zone.

9. Surround Yourself with Inspiration:
- Spend time with people, books, or environments that inspire you. Being in an inspiring environment can naturally lead to taking inspired action.

10. Visualize Success:
- Visualize yourself succeeding in your endeavors. This mental rehearsal can boost your confidence and motivation to take action.

11. Stay Open to Opportunities:
- Be open to unexpected opportunities that may arise. Sometimes, the most inspired actions come from unexpected sources.

12. Practice Gratitude:
- Cultivate an attitude of gratitude. Recognize and appreciate the progress you make and the opportunities that come your way.

13. Review and Adjust:
- Periodically review your goals and actions to ensure they remain aligned with your inspiration and purpose. Adjust your course if necessary.

14. Take Consistent Action:
- Consistency is key to achieving your goals. While inspired actions are important, regular,

disciplined effort is often required to bring your vision to fruition.

15. Celebrate Achievements:
- Celebrate your successes and milestones along the way. Acknowledging your progress can reinforce your motivation and commitment.

16. Create a Vision Board:
- Visual aids like vision boards can help you connect with your goals on a daily basis. Seeing images and words that represent your aspirations can inspire action.

17. Seek Inspiration from Role Models:
- Identify role models or individuals who have achieved what you aspire to accomplish. Learn from their journeys and use their stories as inspiration for your actions.

18. Practice Self-Compassion:
- Be kind to yourself during your journey. Self-compassion can help you overcome self-criticism and fear, making it easier to take inspired action.

19. Journal Your Thoughts and Ideas:
- Keep a journal to capture your thoughts, ideas, and inspirations. Reviewing your journal can help you identify patterns and recurring themes that guide your actions.

20. Stay Open to Learning:
- Be open to acquiring new knowledge and skills related to your goals. Continuous learning can boost your confidence and inspire further action.

21. Find an Accountability Partner:
- Partner with someone who shares your goals or aspirations. An accountability partner can help keep you motivated and on track.

22. Engage in Creative Activities:
- Creative activities, such as writing, painting, or playing music, can tap into your inner inspiration. Engaging in these activities can lead to clarity and motivation.

23. Practice Visualization:
- Visualization exercises can help you see yourself taking the inspired actions required to achieve your goals. This mental rehearsal can strengthen your commitment.

24. Embrace Failure as a Learning Opportunity:
- Understand that setbacks and failures are part of any journey. Instead of seeing them as roadblocks, view them as valuable learning experiences that can guide your future actions.

25. Stay Persistent:
- Persistence is often the key to success. Keep moving forward, even when you encounter

challenges or obstacles. Remember that each step you take brings you closer to your goal.

26. Share Your Journey:
- Sharing your journey with others can provide additional motivation and accountability. It can also inspire those around you to take their own inspired actions.

27. Practice Gratitude:
- Express gratitude for the inspiration and opportunities that come your way. A grateful mindset can attract more positive circumstances and actions.

28. Reconnect with Your Why:
- Periodically revisit your reasons for pursuing your goals. Reconnecting with your "why" can reignite your passion and commitment.

29. Trust the Process:
- Trust that your inspired actions will lead you in the right direction. Have faith in your ability to navigate challenges and stay true to your path.

30. Celebrate Your Growth:
- Recognize and celebrate the personal growth and transformation that occur along the way. These moments of growth are often as meaningful as achieving the end goal.

Taking inspired action is not a one-time event but a way of living. It involves continually seeking and acting on inspiration to create a life that aligns with your values and aspirations. As you consistently apply these principles, you'll find that taking inspired action becomes a natural part of your journey toward personal growth and fulfillment.

❖ Embracing a Life of Flourishing and Beauty: Nurturing Your Inner Garden

Embracing a life of flourishing and beauty is akin to tending to a vibrant and thriving inner garden. It's a journey that involves nurturing your physical, emotional, and spiritual well-being to cultivate a life filled with meaning, joy, and fulfillment. Here's a guide to help you embrace such a life:

Cultivate Self-Love

- *Start by nurturing a deep sense of self-love and self-acceptance. Recognize your inherent worthiness and practice self-compassion.*

Prioritize Well-Being

- *Place a high priority on your physical health. Engage in regular exercise, eat nourishing foods, get enough sleep, and manage stress effectively.*

Practice Mindfulness

- *Incorporate mindfulness into your daily routine. Mindfulness helps you stay present, reduce anxiety, and appreciate the beauty in each moment.*

Build Meaningful Relationships

- *Cultivate and cherish meaningful relationships with friends and family. Foster connections that bring joy, support, and love into your life.*

Pursue Passions

- Identify your passions and interests, and make time for them. Engaging in activities you love adds depth and beauty to your life.

Set and Achieve Goals

- *Set meaningful goals that align with your values. Achieving these goals can provide a sense of accomplishment and purpose.*

Embrace Gratitude

- *Practice gratitude daily. Acknowledging the blessings in your life enhances your appreciation for its beauty.*

Connect with Nature

- *Spend time in nature to connect with its profound beauty. Nature has a way of rejuvenating the soul and instilling a sense of wonder.*

Seek Inner Peace

- *Prioritize your emotional well-being by finding inner peace. Techniques like meditation, journaling, or therapy can help you navigate challenges and find serenity.*

Embody Authenticity

- Embrace your authentic self and live in alignment with your values and beliefs. Authenticity adds depth and beauty to your character.

Explore Spirituality

- *Explore your spiritual beliefs and practices. Many find spiritual connections to be a source of beauty, meaning, and inner peace.*

Give Back and Serve Others

- Acts of kindness and service to others can bring a sense of fulfillment and beauty to your life. Contributing to the well-being of others fosters a deep sense of purpose.

Celebrate Life's Joys

- *Celebrate life's small and significant joys. It's often the little moments of beauty that add richness to your days.*

Practice Forgiveness

- *Release grudges and practice forgiveness. Forgiveness frees you from the burden of negativity, allowing you to experience inner beauty.*

Stay Curious and Learn

- *Cultivate a curious mind and a love for learning. Exploring new ideas and perspectives enriches your understanding of the world.*

Embrace Change

- *Recognize that change is a natural part of life. Embracing change with openness and adaptability can lead to new opportunities and growth.*

Reflect and Journal

- *Regularly reflect on your life journey. Journaling can help you explore your thoughts, feelings, and experiences, leading to personal growth.*

Practice Self-Care

- *Prioritize self-care practices that rejuvenate your mind, body, and soul. This includes activities like spa days, reading, or simply taking time for yourself.*

Be Present for Others

- *Be fully present when you engage with others. Active listening and genuine connections enhance the beauty of your interactions.*

Cultivate Resilience

- *Develop resilience to navigate life's challenges. Viewing challenges as opportunities for growth can add depth to your life story.*

Practice Self-Expression

- *Explore creative outlets like art, writing, music, or dance. Self-expression allows you to convey your inner beauty and emotions.*

Seek Inspiration from Art and Culture

- *Engage with art, literature, music, and cultural experiences that resonate with you. These forms of expression can inspire creativity and appreciation for beauty.*

Find Balance

- *Strive for balance in all areas of your life, including work, relationships, and leisure. Balance promotes overall well-being and harmony.*

Live with Gratitude

- *Develop a daily gratitude practice to remind yourself of the beauty in your life. Gratitude enhances your perspective and fosters positivity.*

Embrace Challenges as Growth Opportunities

- *Instead of fearing challenges, view them as opportunities for personal growth. Overcoming obstacles adds depth to your character.*

Connect with Your Passions

- *Dive deep into your passions and immerse yourself fully in activities that bring you joy. Passion infuses life with beauty and purpose.*

Keep a Beauty Journal

- *Start a journal where you record moments of beauty you encounter in everyday life. Reflecting on these moments can be a source of inspiration.*

Practice Random Acts of Kindness

- *Engage in random acts of kindness to bring beauty to the lives of others. Acts of generosity create ripples of positivity.*

Travel and Explore

- *Travel and explore new places and cultures. Exposure to diverse experiences can broaden your perspective and enrich your life.*

Foster Inner Peace

- *Cultivate inner peace through practices like meditation, deep breathing, or spending time in serene environments. Inner peace enhances your inner beauty.*

Let Go of Judgment

- *Release judgments and criticisms, both of yourself and others. Embracing acceptance and compassion enhances the beauty of your interactions.*

Surround Yourself with Beauty

- *Create a living space that reflects your aesthetic preferences. Surrounding yourself with beauty at home can uplift your spirits.*

Share Your Talents

- *Share your talents and gifts with the world. Your unique abilities contribute to the beauty and richness of the collective human experience.*

Cultivate Positivity

- *Cultivate a positive mindset by focusing on what's going well in your life. Positivity attracts more beauty and abundance.*

Learn from Adversity

- *Embrace adversity as a teacher. The lessons learned during challenging times can lead to profound personal growth and resilience.*

Engage in Acts of Self-Kindness

- *Treat yourself with kindness and self-compassion. Self-kindness nurtures inner beauty and self-worth.*

Practice Active Listening

- *When engaging in conversations, practice active listening. Truly hearing others' perspectives and stories deepens connections.*

Be in Awe of the Universe

- Take time to gaze at the stars, watch a sunrise, or marvel at the wonders of the universe. *Such moments of awe remind you of the beauty and vastness of the world.*

Reflect on Your Legacy

- *Consider the legacy you wish to leave behind. Living a life of beauty and purpose can leave a lasting impact on others.*

Share Your Journey

- *Share your personal journey of embracing a life of flourishing and beauty with others. Your story can inspire and uplift those around you.*

Embracing a life of flourishing and beauty is an ongoing journey that requires conscious effort and self-compassion. By tending to your inner garden with care and intention, you can create a life filled with meaning, joy, and a deep appreciation for the beauty that surrounds you. It's a journey that celebrates both your individual growth and your connection to the world around you

Chapter Ten

The Beauty That Emerges From Within

Unveiling Your Inner Radiance

By now, it becomes evident that beauty is not solely a superficial attribute but a radiant quality that emanates from within. It's a reflection of our character, spirit, and the love and positivity we carry in our heart.

Here's an exploration of the beauty that emerges from within:

1. Authenticity

Authenticity is beautiful. Embrace your true self, flaws, and all, and let your authenticity shine through. Authenticity attracts others who appreciate and resonate with your realness.

2. Compassion and Kindness:

Acts of kindness and compassion are among the most beautiful things a person can do. Your kindness toward others and yourself creates a ripple effect of beauty in the world.

3. Inner Peace

Inner peace is a serene beauty that radiates tranquility. Cultivate inner peace through practices like meditation, mindfulness, and letting go of attachments.

4. Self-Confidence

Confidence is a magnetic form of beauty. Believe in yourself and your abilities, and others will be drawn to your self-assuredness.

5. Resilience

The ability to bounce back from challenges and adversity is a form of beauty that showcases strength and determination. Resilience is a testament to your inner fortitude.

6. Gratitude

Gratitude has a beauty of its own. When you appreciate the beauty in everyday life, you'll find that beauty multiplies around you.

7. Empathy

Empathy, the ability to understand and share the feelings of others, is a beautiful way to connect with people on a deeper level.

8. Joy and Laughter

Genuine joy and laughter are contagious and bring a radiant beauty to your interactions. They uplift the spirits of those around you.

9. Love and Acceptance

Love, both for yourself and others, is perhaps the most beautiful force in the universe. Love fosters acceptance, forgiveness, and a sense of belonging.

10. Wisdom

Wisdom, gained through life experiences and self-reflection, is a graceful form of beauty that offers guidance and perspective.

11. Respecting Differences

Embrace diversity and respect the differences in others. This acceptance of diversity creates a tapestry of beauty in human relationships.

12. Inner Strength

The inner strength to face challenges with grace and courage is a beautiful testament to your character.

13. Humility

Humility is a quiet beauty that speaks volumes. It's a recognition that we are all interconnected and no one is superior to another.

14. Creativity and Passion

Pursue your creative passions with zeal. Your enthusiasm and creativity are expressions of your inner beauty.

15. Self-Compassion

Treat yourself with the same kindness and compassion you offer to others. Self-compassion enhances your inner beauty.

16. Altruism

Acts of selflessness and altruism are a profound form of beauty. They show your capacity to make the world a better place.

17. Mindful Presence

Being fully present in each moment is a form of beauty that allows you to savor life's richness.

18. Forgiveness

Forgiving others and releasing grudges is a beautiful act of letting go and healing.

19. Growth and Evolution

Embrace personal growth and the evolution of your character. Change and growth are part of life's beauty.

20. Living with Purpose

Living with purpose gives your life direction and depth. Purpose infuses your actions with a sense of meaning and beauty.

The beauty that emerges from within is not subject to the passage of time or external circumstances. It is a timeless and enduring beauty that can light up your life and the lives of those around you. As you nurture and cultivate these inner qualities, you'll find that your inner radiance shines brightly, illuminating your path and creating a more beautiful world for all.

Daily Affirmation

Daily affirmation to add to your collections.

Daily affirmations can be a powerful tool for boosting your self-confidence, maintaining a positive mindset, and enhancing your overall well-being. Here's a daily affirmation to help you start your day on a positive note:

"I am resilient and strong, capable of overcoming any challenges that come my way. I embrace my vulnerabilities as a source of growth and connection. I write my own story, turning setbacks into comebacks and failures into opportunities. Today, I choose to believe in myself, find joy in the journey, and radiate the beauty that comes from within."

"I am fearfully and wonderfully made, just as the Bible tells me in Psalm 139:14. I trust in my unique qualities and embrace them as gifts from a loving Creator. I am resilient, for 'I can do all things through Christ who strengthens me' (Philippians 4:13). I release any doubts or fears and replace them with the faith that 'with God, all things are possible' (Matthew 19:26). Today, I choose to live in alignment with my divine purpose, radiating the beauty that God has placed within me."

"I am the architect of my life, and I choose to build a strong and resilient foundation. I embrace change as an opportunity for growth and transformation. I release any doubts or fears that hold me back and replace them with confidence and courage. I am a beacon of positivity, attracting joy, abundance, and love into my life. Today and every day, I choose to shine brightly from within."

"I am a vessel of God's love and grace. Just as Romans 8:28 assures me that 'all things work together for good to those who love God,' I trust that even challenges and setbacks are part of His divine plan for my growth. I am resilient, for 'God is my

refuge and strength, an ever-present help in trouble' (Psalm 46:1). Today, I choose to align with His guidance and purpose, shining my inner light as a testament to His grace."

"I am a source of inspiration and resilience. I trust in my ability to navigate life's challenges with grace and strength. I let go of all negativity and focus on the possibilities that lie ahead. I am open to new opportunities, and I attract positivity into my life effortlessly. Each day is a new chance to grow, learn, and shine my inner beauty even brighter."

"I am the author of my destiny, and I craft a life filled with purpose and joy. I embrace every experience, whether it's a triumph or a challenge, as an opportunity for growth. I radiate love and kindness, nurturing meaningful connections with others. I am a beacon of positivity, and my resilience knows no bounds. Today, I choose to live authentically and manifest my true beauty from within."

"I am a masterpiece in progress, and each day is a new stroke of brilliance. I trust in my ability to navigate life's twists and turns with grace and resilience. I let go of past regrets and embrace the limitless possibilities of the present. I am a magnet for positivity, attracting abundance, happiness, and fulfillment into my life. Today, I choose to shine my inner light even brighter and radiate true beauty."

Feel free to adapt this affirmation to your personal needs and preferences, and repeat it to yourself each morning to set a positive tone for your day. Affirmations are most effective when practiced consistently, so make them a part of your daily routine to reap the benefits over time.

Author Journey from Ashes to True Beauty

Hello reader, my name is Moji Balogun, the author of "Beauty from Ashes" I hope this book has been a source of inspiration to you and you're ready for a New change and a New you!

Before you leave this page, allow me to share my journey on how I rose from ashes to beauty.

Growing up in Lagos, Nigeria, as the child of a single mother, I was no stranger to hardship. Life wasn't easy, and I often wondered why it seemed unfair. But my mother instilled in me the value of words and their incredible power. While others saw adversity, I saw opportunities. Where they saw weakness, I discovered strength.

At a young age, my curiosity and love for books set me apart. I was the kid who would choose a book over toys any day. My mother recognized my potential and knew that I was destined for greatness. However, circumstances forced her to send me to live with my aunt, who had a different plan.

My aunt believed that I wasn't meant for education and refused to send me to school. Instead, she expected me to serve her family as a maid. Those years were tough, marked by physical abuse and a denial of the education I deserved. I missed out on foundational learning experiences that would shape a child's future.

Eventually, my mother rescued me from that challenging situation, but I had fallen behind in my education. But, I determined not to give up, I embarked on a journey of self-learning while also helping my mother with street hawking to make ends meet. It was hard, but I was resolute in my pursuit of knowledge.

The environment around me was far from ideal, with many young people falling into the trap of drugs. Still, I remained steadfast in my determination to break the cycle. As a teenager, I struggled with anger and got into fights, causing trouble in the neighborhood. But even in those turbulent times, my determination to succeed burned bright.

I found solace and purpose in sports. Becoming an athlete allowed me to channel my energy positively. I excelled in sports, representing my school and eventually my state, Lagos State. Medals and accolades became my companions, and I learned the value of hard work and dedication.

In 1984, fate smiled upon me when I met my future husband, my best friend. We met at the National Stadium where we offered training. He moved to the UK after his schooling, and he later sent for me. I joined my husband in 1989 and leading to our marriage in 1994 we were blessed with three beautiful children, and a new chapter of my life began in the UK, full of hope and inspiration.

One of my deepest passions was to become an author, but fear, self-doubt, and anxiety held me back for years. It took two decades to muster the courage to publish my first book – "Beauty from Ashes" a testament to my unwavering belief in never giving up.

My journey is a living testament to the resilience of the human spirit. It's a story of rising from the ashes, conquering inner demons, and embracing the true beauty that lies within. Through determination, and an unshakable commitment to my dreams, I found the strength to overcome life's challenges and create a path filled with resilience, inspiration, and hard work.

As I settled into life in the UK, I realized that a new world of possibilities awaited me. The challenges I had faced in Nigeria had only strengthened my resolve to pursue my dreams. Writing had always been a passion that simmered beneath the surface, and it was time to bring it to the forefront.

However, the path to becoming an author was far from smooth. Self-doubt and fear of failure plagued me. The nagging voices of self-sabotage whispered that I wasn't good enough and that my dreams were unattainable.

Anxiety and depression threatened to overshadow my aspirations.

But here's where the story takes an interesting turn. I decided to confront these inner demons head-on. I began a journey of self-discovery, digging deep into the recesses of my mind to unearth my true potential. It was a courageous leap into the unknown, fuelled by a desire to silence those doubting voices.

Overcoming depression became a pivotal moment in my life. I sought professional help and embarked on a path of healing. It was a journey that required immense self-love and acceptance. I learned that my past did not define me, and I had the power to rewrite my narrative.

As I worked through my struggles, I found humor to be a valuable companion. Laughter became a tool to combat the darkness, and I discovered that even in the most challenging moments, there was room for a smile. It was a reminder that resilience could coexist with joy.

Now, picture this: A young girl, me, balancing stacks of hand-me-down clothes taller than her, trying to strut down the street like a fashion model. Yes, those were my delightful treasures, and I wore them with all the confidence of a runway superstar. Who needed brand-name clothes when you had an eclectic collection of hand-me-downs that could rival any high-fashion wardrobe?

But my journey wasn't all about fashion statements. Oh no, I had a side hustle that would put any entrepreneur to shame. Picture me as a young scavenger, on a quest for hidden treasures in the local dumping ground. You see, recycling wasn't just about saving the planet; it was about filling my pockets with a few extra coins. And hey, who knew that digging through discarded items could be such an adventure?

Now, let's fast forward to my teenage years. Imagine a fiery young girl, fueled by equal parts determination and teenage angst, ready to take on the world. Well, that might be a bit of an exaggeration, but I certainly thought I was invincible. I was the neighborhood's self-appointed superhero, solving disputes with my fists faster than you could say "superhero landing."

But even superheroes have their kryptonite, and mine was education. Thanks to my aunt's dubious parenting choices, I missed out on foundational learning experiences. It was like trying to build a skyscraper without a solid foundation – not the easiest task, let me tell you.

Despite the odds stacked against me, I was determined to catch up. Picture me burning the midnight oil, cramming lessons like my life depended on it. I was on a mission, and nothing could stop me, not even the fact that I was juggling street hawking with my studies.

Now, let's not forget the real hero of this story – my husband. Our love story? Well, it's a classic tale of friendship turning into romance, with a dash of long-distance romance thrown in. He was my best friend, my confidant, and the one who saw the potential in me when I couldn't see it in myself. They say behind every successful person is a supportive partner, and I couldn't agree more.

As life led me to the UK, I found myself in a land of opportunity, far removed from the challenges of my past. But there was one dream that had been simmering beneath the surface for far too long – becoming an author. The only problem? A laundry list of self-doubt, including the infamous "imposter syndrome," which made me question if I could ever be a writer.

But as they say, "When life gives you lemons, make lemonade." So, I decided to turn those lemons into a refreshing glass of self-belief. With humor as my shield and determination as my sword, I faced my inner demons head-on. And guess what? I came out on the other side, not only as an author but as a testament to the power of resilience, humor, and the pursuit of one's dreams.

So, there you have it, a story sprinkled with humor, resilience, and a dash of fashion flair. Because life, as it turns out, is a lot like my hand-me-down clothes – sometimes quirky, often unexpected, but always filled with the potential for a good laugh.

With newfound confidence and a resilient spirit, I finally took the leap to publish my first book. It was a moment of triumph, proof that I could conquer my fears and pursue my dreams despite the odds. The book was a testament to my journey, filled with inspiration and hard-won wisdom.

But the story doesn't end there. It's a story that continues to evolve, with each chapter filled with self-discovery, courage, and the unwavering belief that we can overcome any obstacle. It's a story that celebrates the beauty that emerges from within, even in the face of adversity.

My life's journey is a testament to the power of never giving up, of embracing one's true self, and of finding inspiration in the most unexpected places. It's a story that I hope will inspire others to embark on their own journeys of self-discovery, resilience, and transformation. After all, life may present us with challenges, but it's our response to those challenges that defines our true beauty and strength.

So, as I continue to write the chapters of my life, I do so with a heart filled with gratitude for the lessons learned, the challenges overcome, and the beauty that has emerged from the ashes of adversity. And I invite you, dear reader, to embrace your own journey, knowing that within you lies the power to rise strong and shine brightly, no matter the obstacles you may face.

Indeed, thank goodness for my mother! She's the unsung hero of my story, the rock on which I've built my resilience, and the source of unwavering love and support. Without her strength and guidance, I wouldn't have had the foundation to rise from the ashes and discover my true beauty.

My mother's love and sacrifice shaped my early years. She faced incredible challenges as a single parent, yet she never wavered in her determination to provide for our family. Her resilience in the face of adversity set a powerful example for me, showing me that no obstacle is too great to overcome.

I owe my passion for education to her. She recognized my potential from a young age and did everything in her power to ensure that I had the opportunity to learn and grow. Even when circumstances led me down a difficult path, she remained my guiding light, reminding me of the importance of knowledge and self-improvement.

As I faced hardships and setbacks, it was my mother's unwavering belief in me that kept me going. Her words of encouragement and love were a constant source of strength. She taught me the value of resilience, showing me that it's not about how many times you fall but how many times you get back up.

So, thank God for my mother, the woman who instilled in me the power of resilience and the importance of never giving up. Her love, sacrifice, and unwavering support are the threads that weave through the tapestry of my life, guiding me on my journey from ashes to true beauty.

Finally, I am a reflection of God's grace and love. I trust that He has equipped me with the strength to face any challenges that come my way. Just as it is written in Philippians 4:13, 'I can do all things through Christ who strengthens me,' I know that His divine guidance and presence empower me to overcome adversity. Today, I choose to walk in His light and manifest my true beauty as a testament to His glory.

I thank God for this incredible journey I've undertaken. I am grateful for every experience, both the challenges and the triumphs, as they have shaped me into who I am today. I trust in His divine plan for my life, knowing that every step has been guided by His wisdom and love. Today, I celebrate the beauty that has emerged from within, and I look forward to the continued growth and blessings that lie ahead.

In closing, I invite you to embark on your own journey from ashes to true beauty, for within each of us lies the power to rise strong, embrace our vulnerabilities, and craft a future filled with resilience and beauty.

It's a journey that requires courage, self-discovery, and the willingness to confront our inner demons. But remember, it's in those moments of vulnerability and self-reflection that we find our greatest strength.

So, I challenge you to:

1. Embrace Your Vulnerabilities: Don't be afraid to acknowledge your weaknesses and insecurities. It's through vulnerability that we connect with others on a deeper level and find the strength to overcome.
2. Write Your Own Story: Take ownership of your narrative. You have the power to turn setbacks into comebacks, failures into successes, and heartbreak into healing. Your story is uniquely yours, and it's waiting to be written.
3. Seek Support and Help: Don't hesitate to reach out for support when you need it. Whether it's from friends, family, or professionals, seeking help is a sign of strength, not weakness.

4. Cultivate Resilience: Understand that resilience is a skill that can be developed over time. It's about bouncing back, learning from adversity, and growing stronger with each challenge.
5. Embrace Self-Discovery: Get to know yourself on a deeper level. Explore your passions, dreams, and desires. Rediscover what makes you truly happy and fulfilled.
6. Practice Forgiveness: Forgive not only others but also yourself. Holding onto grudges and self-blame only weighs you down. Let go of the past and make room for a brighter future.
7. Find Purpose and Meaning: Seek out what brings meaning to your life. Whether it's through your career, hobbies, or helping others, finding purpose can be a powerful motivator.
8. Connect with Your Spirituality: Explore your spiritual beliefs and how they can provide strength and guidance in your journey. Spirituality can be a source of inner peace and resilience.
9. Build Self-Esteem and Self-Worth: Recognize your inherent value and worthiness. You are enough just as you are, and you deserve love, respect, and happiness.
10. Set Goals for Personal Transformation: Define your aspirations and create a roadmap for personal growth. Setting and achieving goals can be incredibly empowering.

Remember, the journey from ashes to true beauty is not a straight path but a winding road filled with twists and turns. Embrace the process, celebrate your victories, and learn from your challenges. And above all, never give up on yourself, for your true beauty emerges from the depths of your resilience and the authenticity of your story.

So, are you ready to embark on this transformative journey? The call to action is yours to answer, and the beauty that awaits you is boundless.

www.ingramcontent.com/pod-product-compliance
Lightning Source LLC
LaVergne TN
LVHW061613070526
838199LV00078B/7262